Nurturing the

write

Relationship

**Developing a Family Writing Lifestyle
and Traditions**

by

Mary Ann Froehlich

Nurturing the Write Relationship
Developing a Family Writing Lifestyle and Traditions
By Mary Ann Froehlich. Foreword by Robin Sampson

© Copyright June 2007
All Rights Reserved

ISBN-10: 0970181698
ISBN-13: 978-0970181695

Heart of Wisdom Publishing Inc
146 Chriswood Lane
Stafford, VA 22556

www.heartofwisdom.com

Printed in the United States of America
Unless otherwise indicated, all Bible verses are from the KJV and
used by permission (Eph 6:17)

BOOKS BY MARY ANN FROEHLICH

What's a Smart Woman Like You Doing in a Place Like This?

Music Education in the Christian Home

An Early Journey Home:
Helping Families Work Through the Loss of a Child

Holding Down the Fort:
Help and Encouragement for Wives Whose Husbands Travel*

Music Therapy with Hospitalized Children:
A Creative Arts Child Life Approach

What to Do When You Don't Know What to Say*

What to Do When You Don't Know
What to Say to Your Own Family*

101 Ideas for Piano Group Class:
Building an Inclusive Music Community
for Students of All Ages and Abilities

Facing the Empty Nest:
Avoiding a Midlife Meltdown When Your Child Leaves Home

Nurturing the WRITE Relationship:
Developing a Family Writing Lifestyle and Traditions

*Coauthored with PeggySue Wells

Table of Contents

Dedicated to

Suzanne,

Janelle, Natalie,

and Maria,

for making the writing process magical.

Magical writing is contagious.
Lucy Calkins

Acknowledgements

With many thanks to:

—Robin Sampson and her staff at Heart of Wisdom Publishing for
  bringing this project to completion.

—John for his love and tangible support.

—Suzanne, Janelle, Erin, Kristine, Tracy, Michael, and Craig
  for allowing me to be part of their extraordinary writing group.

—PeggySue Wells for her partnership in writing the *What to Do When
  You Don't Know What to Say* series and other ideas she has inspired in
  this book.

Foreword
by Robin Sampson

As an author, publisher, homeschool mother, and educator, I am thrilled to see the completion of this book. I was excited as soon as I saw the words "A Family Writing Lifestyle." Mary Ann shares valuable insights not only about writing itself, but about passing on the gift of written expression as a family tradition. What a gift to pass on to your children —the ability to capture insights, record memories, and relate perceptions and feelings.

We have eleven children ages 5 to 34. I have always encouraged my children to write. Almost twenty years ago, when we began our homeschool journey, teaching my children to write well was one of my main goals. The years of writing encouragement have paid off. All my grown children write regularly. Even my very busy 32-year old daughter (a mother of five) finds time to relate touching thoughts and memories through her family scrapbook journaling. Now I take pleasure in priceless annotated scrapbook pages of my grandchildren. I continue to encourage my youngest children to write daily. My five-year old loves to dictate his fascinating stories as I record them. My seven-year old son enjoys copywork and writing and illustrating letters to servicemen. He has written or dictated stories about horses, baseball, and knights (the same type of writing his 28-year old brother wrote when he was seven).

The importance of teaching your children to write cannot be overstated. Skillful writers influence society. Christian writers have the privilege of encouraging, teaching, and strengthening others to have a closer relationship with God. The late Dr. Paul Bubna, former President of the Christian and Missionary Alliance, wrote, "It may be true that a picture is worth a thousand words, but we must not miss the fact that writing words has a unique power all its own. Something powerful happens to the person who writes the words. It is one thing to think the thought, it is quite another to put it into words and see it on paper, or even a computer screen. That process opens a door of intimacy with one's self that may be unmatched any other way." Our spiritual lives, our success in the work world, and our social networks all require the skill of writing. Writing skills are vital in today's changing culture. Written communication declined during the age of the telephone but with the development of the computer people are writing again in the form of emails and blogging (online journaling).

In my book, *A Heart of Wisdom Teaching Approach*, I encourage parents to teach their children to write to learn, also known as writing across the curriculum. Mary Ann embraces the same concept because she understands how writing helps to generate thoughts and to organize them logically and concisely. Writing can bring experiences, thoughts, and opinions together. We write to express ideas, share stories, document history, imagine the future, express love, and dispense humor. When students tackle a subject, they can experiment with different techniques and strategies for writing. They discover new ideas, new ways of thinking, and new methods of expressing themselves. When you teach your children to document their thoughts, feelings, and ideas on paper, you are equipping them with a gift they will use for a lifetime. Mary Ann demonstrates the practical steps to develop this type of writing into a family lifestyle.

This book will be a useful guide for any teacher and especially beneficial to homeschoolers. Most homeschoolers are fond of Charlotte Mason's educational philosophies which emphasize real-life activities over academic exercises. Mary Ann agrees with Mason explaining how writing assignments that are viewed as academic exercises cause the child to lose the adventure of writing. Mason's admirers will appreciate how Mary Ann's unique approach is in agreement with Mason's philosophy "… we believe that childrens' minds are capable of digesting real knowledge, so we provide a rich, generous curriculum that exposes children to many interesting, living ideas and concepts." Mary Ann will show you how families working on individual and joint writing projects can motivate children to catch the excitement of relevant writing and come to understand that the art of writing is a powerful life tool.

I became eager to try out Mary Ann's methods when I read how she taught her children to write using a real-life approach following the rules of an adult writing group. She posed as a mock publisher to lead her children through the writing process from query letters to contracts and finished publications, complete with book signings, and marketing techniques. What a great idea! About a dozen years ago when my grown children were young and learning to write they each created a book using *Creating Books with Children* by Valerie Bendt as a guide. Through the creation of their books they learned the writing, illustrating, editing processes but they never learned the query and submission processes . Here we are over a decade later writing again, with my youngest children, using Mary Ann's ideas. I look forward to adding more finished writing products to my somewhat yellowed and faded but treasured papers of childhood thoughts, stories, inspiration, opinions, and beliefs to our family files.

Although Mary Ann emphasizes forming a writing group, this is only one segment of her collection of ideas. This book contains much more. You will also learn how writing activities and rituals can be woven through the day, year, and even throughout life. Activities include ideas for family journaling, letter writing, Bible journaling, goal journaling, celebration journaling, apology letters, thank-you notes, and even writing to deal with loss and grief. This book is not about the educational nuts and bolts of writing, but is intended to celebrate and inspire writing in the home. *Nurturing the WRITE Relationship* will help you develop a family writing lifestyle and tradition.

  • Section I teaches you the importance of creating a safe place to write, allowing children to experiment with language. Children will become confident writers when they receive support and encouragement as they move through the writing process.

  • Section II details writing education principles. Mary Ann explains how to learn from great writers and how to be a writing mentor to your children. She also dispels several writing myths.

  • Section III explains the publishing process for a writing group from vision to revision to the completed process.

• Section IV encourages teaching children through journaling, brainstorming, contract and letter writing, and other formats.

• Section V encourages you to develop a family writing lifestyle with family rituals, traditions, and celebrations and investigates a Biblical view of writing.

• Section VI includes many ideas for integrating writing into daily life and closes with the twelve writing principles of a family writing lifestyle.

Mary Ann's book is full of several first-rate unique ideas to teach children to write that make writing a fun family experience. She provides an attractive combination of solid advice and clever insights on how to motivate and cultivate your children's writing. I'm giving this book to each of my grown children to support them in their efforts to teach their children to write. I hope your family will spend time developing a family writing lifestyle. I promise it will be time well spent and the benefits are many.

Robin Sampson
heartofwisdom.com/blog

The right to write is a birthright, a spiritual dowry that gives us the keys to the kingdom.

Julia Cameron

I begin with the first sentence and trust to Almighty God for the second.

Laurence Sterne

Chapter 1

Introduction:
Why Did I Write This Book?

Writing is an exploration.
You start from nothing and learn as you go.

E. L. Doctorow

I never intended to write this book. My children had actually groaned through the years as I asked them to participate in dinner table writing games. My husband, who hates to write, and children had laughed at me, constantly making fun of my unusual pen-to-paper traditions. Sometimes they would invite their friends to our celebrations so they could witness in person how crazy I was. As teenagers, my daughters would even include their boyfriends. Then **everybody** could laugh at me.

Yet my oldest daughter recently asked, "Mom, can you write down all those silly traditions so that we can do them with our kids?" I was shocked…my offspring wanted to continue the craziness? (I never doubted that laughter was the most important part of the process.)

I am writing this book because the strength of traditions lies in passing them on. This book is offered as a gift to my children and grandchildren. As a reader, you are welcome to share the journey with your own family.

The family is a natural writing group, a safe place to encourage a passion for writing. The professional writing group I participated in for ten years was a safe place to share our writing and our lives, encourage one another's projects, as well as develop a joint book project. At the same time I was involved with the adult writers' group, my ten-year-old daughter was invited to join a children's writing group. The young writers enjoyed meeting real-life authors, so their teacher invited me to meet with them and explain the publishing process. Then I thought of a crazy idea which their teacher enthusiastically embraced: I wanted to pose as a mock publisher, to lead the children through the authentic process, from query letters to contracts to finished publications, complete with book signings, interviews, and other marketing techniques. Over the course of one year, these young writers learned how to move from brainstorming ideas to selling a completed product. The publishing process is outlined in Section Three as a model for any writing group to follow.

I knew from my experience as a Suzuki music teacher that when music study is relegated to being an academic subject, children cannot flourish musically. Children do not become fluent musicians by practicing an instrument for thirty minutes a day. Immersion in a musical world, where musical experiences are woven throughout the day in the fabric of children's lives, creates natural musicians, from daily listening to great works of music and attending concerts, to singing and playing instruments with one's family and friends. A musical lifestyle must first be modeled by parents and mentors. Children learn most effectively when they feel that they are honing skills which are relevant and useful in their present daily lives as well as for their future.

Creating fluent writers requires the same immersion. When writing assignments are viewed as academic exercises, the adventure of writing is lost. When families can develop their own writing-group community for working on individual and joint writing projects, children catch the excitement of relevant writing. They come to understand that the art of writing is a powerful life tool. In the chapters to follow, you will see that writing activities and rituals can be woven throughout one's day, year, and even throughout life. More important than developing natural writing skills, however, your family will also experience one of the most tangible ways available to nurture relationships. Expressing ourselves through the written word cannot help but be relational, as we process life's challenges by putting pen to paper.

This book is not about the educational nuts and bolts of teaching writing. I will wisely leave that to the expertise of trained English teachers. This book is intended to celebrate and inspire writing in the home. You will find my favorite quotes about writing inserted between chapters in this book, and Scripture verses in Chapter 15 to use as writing prompts for journaling. Before you can share the adventure of writing with your family, you must experience it yourself. Do not read further until you find a corresponding journal to keep handy as you read the following chapters. Write down your responses to quotes, questions, and verses; brainstorm about ideas for your family, and record flashes of insight. Stop reading and start writing whenever you feel inspired.

Think of *Nurturing the WRITE Relationship* as inspired by a homophone. Homophones are words that sound the same but are spelled in various ways and have different meanings. Some examples are knight/night and meet/meat. This book is based on write, rite, and right. The integration of these words summarizes this book in a nutshell:

- Write Understand the importance of, and develop the use of, the written word.

- Rite Understand the importance of cultivating rituals in family life.

- Right Understand the importance of communication in developing right relationships.

This book is a baton. Our oldest daughter graduates from college this spring, our younger daughter is a college freshman, and our son attends high school. This baton is lovingly handed to you, especially those of you with young children. The bond you cultivate through these writing traditions can build a foundation which will last a lifetime.

Writing rights things.

Julia Cameron

One of the most potent writer's blocks I know is the fear of loneliness that people associate with the writing life.
Not writing is the lonely thing.

Julia Cameron

For me, writing something down was the only road out…
I hated childhood, and spent it sitting behind a book waiting for adulthood to arrive. When I ran out of books I made up my own. At night, when I couldn't sleep, I made up stories in the dark.

Ann Tyler

I started writing when I was five. It never occurred to me that it was something you were supposed to worry about. You learn to write by doing it.

Madeleine L'Engle

Section I

Finding a
Safe Place to Write

Chapter 2

No Safe Place
to Write

The whole duty of a writer is to please and satisfy himself,
and the true writer always plays to an audience of one.

E. B. White

I still remember the knot in my stomach. I dreaded going to school that day in fifth grade.

Our 25-page world geography reports were due. As always, I had become totally lost in the project and written a 565-page novel, complete with dialogue and characters for each country. I never set out to write a lengthy volume…it just happened. But then that fateful day arrived when I needed to bring it to school and face the taunts of my peers. I often tried to hide my writing in my desk, but inevitably the moment would come when our teacher said, "Please hand in your papers."

"Teacher's pet…teacher's pet…you just want to make the rest of us look bad." My classmates' comments haunted me. There was no way for me to explain to them that I simply loved to write. No malice was intended.

There was no safe place to write in school. Having been promoted early in elementary school, I remained the youngest and smallest student in each of my classes. As an only child, I had no older siblings to protect me, and I was easily intimidated by my bigger classmates. Understanding teachers would discreetly excuse me from physical education activities, a daily nightmare where I could not physically compete with my peers, to read books on the sidelines. I would pray that it would rain during recess so we could remain in the classroom to continue working and writing. Yes, I was an odd child. I identify with Katherine Paterson, the Newbery Medal-winning author of children's books, who writes:

> *When people ask me what qualifies me to be a writer for children, I say I was once a child. But I was not only a child, I was, better still, a weird little kid, and though I would never choose to give my own children this particular preparation for life, there are few things, apparently, more helpful to a writer than having once been a weird little kid.*
>
> *I'm sure there are plenty of fine writers who have overcome the disadvantages of a normal childhood and have gone on to do great things. It's just that we weird little kids seem to have a head start.*
>
> Katherine Paterson
> *Gates of Excellence*

Like Katherine Paterson, I found refuge in the world of books and writing. It was my safe retreat, a place where life could be any way I desired. Norton Juster's *The Phantom Tollbooth* was one of my favorite books. I was entranced with the lands named Dictionopolis and Digitopolis. Norton Juster understood those of us who are citizens of Dictionopolis and have a passion for words above all else. Authors and characters were my personal friends.

Something magical and powerful happened when I began writing. To be alone with pen and paper was sheer bliss. I would become totally immersed in the creative process, losing all track of time, similar to my experiences of playing the piano and composing music. I would later learn that this experience is called "flow," a psychological state of surrender. As an adult in an age of technology, I've found the process of putting pen to paper has changed into using a computer, but the magic remains the same. Research and writing were to become my adult passions.

Through reading the biographies of other authors, I have discovered one childhood trait they shared in common—the world of books and writing was their refuge and escape from a hostile world too.

While other students may have discouraged my writing, exceptional teachers encouraged it. My high school honors English teachers were a lifeline for me. These mentors shared their passion for literature. They required us to daily WRITE…WRITE…WRITE…write about our personal experiences, write about what we knew. They emphasized a clear, concise writing style, forever crying to "eliminate the jargon." One experience during my sophomore year stands out.

Our honors class was filled with bright, unusually verbal students. Lively debates about literature were common. Of course, I never said a word. I had learned from past school experiences that staying invisible was my safest coping mechanism. My teacher entered the class one morning and said, "It is time for all of you big-mouths to be quiet for a minute. Sometimes people can write what they cannot say. I want you to listen to an excellent piece of writing." We assumed that she would read a work by one of her favorite authors. I was shocked as she proceeded to read a paper that I had written. The class was silent, and my teacher affirmed me without mentioning my name. Her message was clear—keep writing.

My home was a safe place to write. Writing was part of our lifestyle. Books were everywhere. My mother had been a journalist in her youth. My grandmother had been famous for writing letters so beautiful and profound that they could be framed. Writing to friends, writing thank-you notes, writing at every opportunity was a given in our home. My mother immigrated to the United States as a young person and remained intimate with friends she had not spoken with in decades. They had written letters—not notes, but deep, personal, lengthy conversations on paper. My mother also put love notes in my dad's lunchbox when she prepared his lunch every morning.

I grew up knowing that writing was a critical part of life. It made anything possible. Even today I solve problems by writing. I process life by seeing it on paper.

As much as I enjoyed a lifetime of writing, however, I never intended to become a professional author. That career path took me by surprise. I published my research after graduate school and continued to write for various journals. The articles soon developed into books. Having left my career to become a full-time mother, I realized that the one thing I did not have to give up was writing. It remained a haven for me.

My deficiencies also led me into writing. I was not quick enough on my feet to properly answer questions posed to me, such as: How do you help the family of a terminally ill child? ...What is the best way to develop musicianship in a child? ...What is creative arts therapy? ...How do you handle life when your husband is traveling? ...and more questions. The only way I knew how to effectively answer such questions was through writing, and books resulted.

You can now understand why I was thrilled when my third-grade daughter, Janelle, daily came home from school with news about her writers' workshop. Janelle was learning to research, mindmap, write modern versions of classic fairy tales, and publish her own books to share with classmates. She was reading fine literature, memorizing Shakespearean poetry, and learning about real-life authors.

My daughter was developing a passion for writing. Janelle and I had been writing together at home for years, just as my mother had encouraged me, but it was her teacher, Mrs. Thomas*, who ignited the spark and fanned it into a flame.

The following year, Mrs. Thomas invited Janelle and some other former classmates to join an after-school writing group. It was an opportunity that changed my daughter's life. It was the safe experience that I had craved as a child, to fully explore and enjoy writing with the support of other children. Of course, I could not stay away.

I may still remember the knot in my stomach, but someday my daughter will not.

> *In writing, as in all art, confidence is the beginning of skill.*
> Paul Johnson

*At her request, this teacher's name was changed to protect her privacy.

Questions for Reflection

When you were a child, was school a safe or unsafe place for writing? Was your home a safe or unsafe place for writing?

There are a thousand thoughts lying within a man that he does not know till he takes up the pen to write.

William Thackeray

Stories can change the world. Stories still push back the darkness and bind us together into communities.

Lucy Calkins

One ought to write only when one leaves a piece of one's flesh in the inkpot each time one dips one's pen.

Leo Tolstoi

Chapter 3

A Safe Place to Write:
Introduction to the Writing Group

I needed a place to risk without ridicule.
I was not ready for unkind—let alone savage—critiques.
I'd met them in school and they left me shaking.
I hoped that a freewriting group would be safe.

Ann Cooper
The Writing Group Book

No formula exists for a successful writing group. Writing groups are as individual as the members involved. Some groups are tailored for beginning writers, while others are geared toward professional authors. Some groups are designed for children, while others are for adults. Each group may be unique in its methods, purpose, and format, but all groups have one trait in common: **every writing group is a safe place to write.** It is essentially a support group for writers, no matter the individual flavor.

The craft of writing can be an isolating experience, and the companionship of other writers is both comforting and inspiring. Sometimes we need an encouraging word (or a challenging one). Trust and consistency are essential. We are partners in creating art, accountable to one another.

Writing groups may meet weekly, monthly, or bi-monthly. Most groups operate well with six to eight members. Some groups enjoy planning social events and holiday parties to augment writing sessions; other groups are all business. Writing groups can be structured in a variety of ways. Here are some examples:

- Read and critique (not criticism) groups—Members gather on a regular basis to read work written outside the group and receive feedback from other members.

- Writing practice groups—Members come together to spontaneously write during the actual meeting, using writing prompts and other points of inspiration. Writers are encouraged to read aloud but critiques are not offered. These sessions are for free writing and sharing.

- Writing workshop groups—Members gather for mini-classes on topics about writing. The leader presents new material and helps writers with specific techniques. Guest speakers are invited. Weekend writing retreats can be planned.

- Common experience groups—Members are writing on the same topic, from writers who travel, to those who are living with cancer. These can become informal support groups. Travel writers may arrange trips/writing excursions together.

- Common genre groups—Members explore the same genre: novels, plays, poetry, children's books, autobiographies, fiction, nonfiction, etc.

- Journal-writing groups—Though all writers use journaling as a tool, this type of group focuses on journaling through life's challenges and sharing this process with others in the group.

- Project groups—The group works toward a specific goal, e.g., publishing an anthology of essays or producing a play.

- Women's story circle—Women write their lives' stories, gather to share them with one another, and read the memoirs of other female authors. The focus is the journey that women share, making sense of it through writing.

- Online group—Members "meet" online to share publishing information and critique manuscripts by e-mail.

Some writers are more comfortable in groups with strict guidelines. Perhaps one professional writer is working on the final chapters of a novel contracted to be published soon and needs feedback from other professionals. The read and critique group meets her needs. Other writers may want an integrated approach. A beginning writer who has not been published may want to participate in a group which offers a combination of workshops, writing practice, and critique.

Playwrights may want to meet only with other playwrights who understand their craft. A nonfiction writer may want to be exposed to the workings of poetry and fiction, enriching his own work. Other writers may be looking more for a supportive community and accountability than new techniques. Every writer has individual needs, requiring a unique writers' group format. Anne Lamott calls other writers who we trust to read our work "midwives."

Variations

Writers begin as readers, and words become a means of survival.
Jayne Anne Phillips

Effective writing groups often integrate different approaches. For example, a read and critique group may bring in guest speakers or design a weekend retreat for writing practice experiences. Sometimes groups do not begin with a project in mind but evolve into producers of a group creation, such as a poetry anthology complete with a public reading.

Some groups publish a monthly newsletter. In addition to sharing relevant information, members can be regularly published. Other groups hold writing contests and bestow awards. Some groups enjoy round-robin writing exercises, during which members add to a piece of writing as it goes around the group. One group created a group novel (each member wrote a successive chapter) and it was actually published. Other groups hold weekend retreats to encourage members to write a novel in a weekend.

Groups with seasoned writers may be dedicated to publication. Members attend writing conferences, meet with agents, contact bookstores to arrange book signings and readings, and help each other market their work.

Common Threads

One common thread in most writing groups is the opportunity to socialize and dine together after the writing session. Writers cannot build trust without building relationships.

Setting ground rules at the outset is critical to the success of the group. Two common ground rules are:
—Confidentiality—What is shared in the group does not leave the group.
—Respect—Ideas are never stolen or "borrowed."

Marnie Brooks, in *The Writing Group Book*, lists two rules in her group as:
—Critique the piece, not the person.
—Listen to the critique with mouths shut and ears open.

Other Examples of Writing Groups

There's nothing to writing.
All you do is sit down at a typewriter and open a vein.
Red Smith

My daughter and I have each participated in structured writing groups with different goals. This book is not written for formal writing groups but for families who hope to incorporate an informal writing community into their lifestyle. Ideally, this experience could extend beyond the immediate family to include relatives and friends, depending on the activity.

As you read this chapter, pick and choose from different formats to design your own writing group to meet the needs of your individual family.

Example of a Children's Writing Group

My daughter participated in a writing group with five friends, mentored by their former teacher. They met once a week after school for two years. Cooperative learning principles provided the framework, ensuring a safe community where the children respected and trusted one another.

These young writers participated in a smorgasbord group. Sometimes they wrote during the session, often collaborating with a partner. At other times they discussed their writing process and read to each other. Sometimes their teacher presented material on specific techniques and genres.

Each member was creating a work in a different genre. Participants were also working toward a group goal—publication of their works. One member was writing a play, which culminated in a performance given by the group. Field trips to meet professional authors were organized.

During the first year, the format was fluid and open as the children explored writing and learned to trust one another. The second year brought more structured goals, when the children were comfortable with the writing group process and ready for a new challenge (discussed in Section Three).

Example of a Women's Journal Writing Group

While my daughter was participating in her writing group, I was involved in a very different group. The leader hand picked the members: ten women who enjoyed writing and wanted to chronicle their journeys as mothers who integrated their careers with raising families for ten years. Some writers were published, others were not. We were all different ages. One writer was newly married and pregnant with her first child; other writers were raising teenagers. We met bi-monthly in the beginning, but as members began moving around the country, we met once a year. Some writers dropped out of the group. Other writers lived through painful divorces. The purpose of the group was to record life changes, and our writing certainly mirrored that.

When we met together, we read samples of journal entries written during the previous months. We also discussed our individual writing work and supported one another in completing projects and seeking publishers.

The leader's goal from the outset was clear. She wanted to combine our most significant journal entries into a book which showed how women can approach the challenge of juggling children and a career in radically different ways. Through all the personal changes in the contributors' lives, as well as changes within the writing group, her goal was accomplished. The volume was self-published, dedicated to our children, and released for Mother's Day 2000. With the project finalized, the group disbanded.

We were a common experience group, a read and critique group, a story circle group, and a common project group, but more importantly, we were simply women who found comfort in meeting with other mothers/writers who understood the shared challenges in our lives.

Writing Partnerships and Collaborations

It is not often that someone comes along who is a true friend and a good writer.

E. B. White
Charlotte's Web

Not everyone has time for the luxury of joining a formal writing group. Sometimes a writer only needs one other person (preferably a fellow writer) to hold him or her accountable, commiserate when the rejection letters arrive, critique a difficult passage, discuss potential projects, and simply be a true friend. Children as well as adults need writing buddies. Some writers plan monthly writing dates where the two of them can sit side by side in a café and write for hours. Sometimes writing friendships grow past that point and collaborations take root. Many coauthors began as good friends with common interests.

PeggySue Wells was a journalist who took an interest in my book projects. Her daughter was one of my piano students. PeggySue's husband traveled as much as mine did, so our families often met for pizza when we were "single mothers." One day she said, "I think that we should write a book about living with traveling husbands." Half-joking, half-serious, we realized that many other women were in our position. After *Holding Down the Fort: Encouragement for Wives Whose Husbands Travel* was published, we continued collaborating on other book projects.

PeggySue and I now live on opposite sides of the country and can "meet" only through e-mail and the telephone. We continue to encourage one another as we pursue individual projects. Neither of us went looking for a writing buddy, but have found the benefits of a writing partnership worth the effort invested.

Ideally the writing group, whether it includes two or ten writers, provides a safe environment for writing, where members trust and encourage each other. Formats can be combined, depending on the individual needs of the writers involved. Every writer can benefit from having writing buddies; indeed, a supportive writing community is the foundation of the family writing lifestyle.

> *We find a home for our heart when we are safe*
> *and know our voices will be heard.*
> Charlotte Sophia Kasl

For more information about writing groups, read:
    Writing Alone, Writing Together by Judy Reeves
    The Writing Group Book by Lisa Rosenthal

For writing prompts and inspiration, refer to:
    A Writer's Book of Days by Judy Reeves
    The Writer's Idea Book by Jack Heffron

Questions for Reflection

Envision your ideal writing community.

How would you design a writing group that fits your needs?

Teaching writing is, above all, teaching thinking.
                                            Donald Murray

Everyone is a writer. You are a writer. All over the world, in every culture, human beings have carved into stone, written on parchment, birch bark, or scraps of paper, and sealed into letters—their words. Those who do not write stories and poems on solid surfaces tell them, sing them, and, in so doing, write them on the air. Creating with words is our continuing passion. We dream stories; we make up stories, poems, songs, and tell them to ourselves. All alone, we write.

                                            Pat Schneider

That's not what writing is—writing what you know. You write in order to find things out.
                                            Garrison Keillor

Section II

Writing Education Principles

Chapter 4

Learning from Great Writing Teachers:
Research as Our Foundation

Writing is fostered, not taught.
                                        Frank Smith

The key to developing young writers is creating an environment where writing can naturally flourish. Writing is first a natural creative act. Cross-brain activities and cultivating the imagination are keys to effective education. Writing is an artistic endeavor.

Imagination is power. Artists are creators, and art is the realization of worlds that we all have the potential of creating. Creating is a fundamental and continual urge, and it is a restriction on human potential that so few people do it.

                                        Frank Smith
                                        to think

The following principles are our foundation, based on research and the proven methods of effective writing teachers. I encourage you to personally read these authors' contributions (listed in the bibliography), but I have summarized ten principles common to each. Be patient as you wade through the material because it undergirds the family writing lifestyle.

These principles can be applied in the home, classroom, or writing group. I have personally witnessed these principles being applied in classrooms, so I know it is possible. Yet I realize now how exceptional our family's experience was.

My children's elementary school classrooms were alive with the celebration of learning. They were supportive, safe places to develop a passion for reading and writing. Their teachers were trained in cooperative learning, integrated thematic instruction, the Writers' Workshop model, and brain-compatible research, to name a few of their areas of expertise. The results were phenomenal. My children could not wait to go to school every day. Unfortunately, some children dread going to school. As I would rave about our public school teachers, my friends would stare in disbelief.

The pioneering writing teachers that you will be introduced to have been called the "ripples of resistance" by Frank Smith, because they teach young writers the way they naturally learn. They listened to their students and learned from them.

> *The teaching of writing is a very Socratic kind of teaching and*
> *you should stay out of the people's way rather than get in it.*
> Wallace Stegner
> *On Teaching and Writing Fiction*

Principle 1

Learning to write should be a brain-compatible experience.

> *Engage the learner joyfully and you will get results.*
> Eric Jensen

Children learn when they are engaged. Our challenge is to engage young writers, based on our understanding of how the brain functions.

Cross-modal learning...left/right brain hemispheres...the triune brain...the theory of multiple intelligences...neurodevelopmental systems...we are familiar with these terms. Brain researchers have each made significant contributions to learning theory. When I was studying to become a music therapist almost thirty years ago, cross-modal learning was the new focus. Successful learning activities targeted auditory, kinesthetic, visual, tactile, cognitive, and social areas. Crossover activities integrated learning on both sides of the brain. Today these approaches are widely accepted, with varied names.

Dr. Leslie Hart, a champion for brain-compatible activities for children, views linear activities as brain-antagonistic. They do not lead the brain down the path it naturally proceeds. The brain simultaneously processes along many paths, and thus is more complex than our original understanding of left/right brain hemispheres. Engaged learning occurs when multiple brain sites are connected.

Dr. Howard Gardner identifies seven multiple intelligences or problem solving capabilities: verbal/linguistic, logical-mathematical, visual/spatial, body/kinesthetic, musical/rhythmic, and interpersonal and intrapersonal. The more avenues children can target, the more effectively they learn and adapt.

Dr. Mel Levine describes these functions as eight neurodevelopmental systems: attention control, memory, language, motor, higher thinking, social, spatial, and sequential ordering.

If you can only read one book about brain functions, read Levine's *A Mind at a Time*. He describes our minds as tool chests, filled with delicate instruments to learn and perform tasks. These instruments, neurodevelopmental systems, combine as clusters. Each brain is uniquely wired, with its own specialized systems. Every human being can benefit from understanding his or her neurodevelopmental profile. Levine encourages teachers to teach the way the brain learns. More importantly, teachers must adapt their instruction to the way that **individual** brains learn.

The enemies of brain-compatible learning are anxiety and fear. When students feel judged, stressed, or threatened in any way, they cannot learn. Proster theory is based on the triune brain concept. Dr. Paul MacLean described the brain as consisting of three partners: the brain stem, the limbic system, and the cerebral cortex. Learning and problem solving occur in the cerebral cortex. The limbic system connects cognitive and emotional centers. The brain stem is responsible for survival. When we feel threatened, our brain downshifts to a survival mode, freezing our ability to adapt and learn. We shut down.

Children and adults cannot learn a new skill without taking risks. Students who are afraid to fail will not take risks.

Teachers often ask psychologists how to motivate children to learn.
The answer is to make it safe for them to risk failure.
To welcome mistakes is to encourage learning.
Haim Ginott

Dr. Frank Smith and Dr. Gabriele Lusser Rico are leading researchers on brain-compatible learning and the writing process. Dr. Rico, author of *Writing the Natural Way*, states that any creative product must be a collaboration of the two brain hemispheres. Effective teaching accesses the whole brain. Writing can produce the joyful result of flowing with our natural brain process or the tragic result of fighting against it.

Perfectionism is the voice of the oppressor, the enemy of the people.
Perfectionism will ruin your writing...
Anne Lamott
Bird by Bird: Some Instructions on Writing and Life

Rico believes that children are natural poets. Right-brain dominance in early childhood is evidenced by such natural traits as wonder, playfulness, spontaneity, surprise, delight, willingness to take risks, fascination with sounds, creativity, a rich imagination, and storytelling. Traditional left-brain education suppresses the right brain and inhibits creative thinking.

Rico's method of accessing both brains in writers is called *clustering*, similar to Tony Buzan's popular process of mindmapping, which has been applied to the business field as well as education and therapy. Both encourage free-flow thinking on paper, without analysis or judgment (which block the creative process).

To be successful, the writing process must be a neural networking experience.

Imagination is the basis of reality, and the brain that cannot exercise creative thought is the one in which imagination has been constrained and shackled. It is as natural for the brain to invent as it is for muscles to move.
Frank Smith
Writing and the Writer

Principle 2

A traditional focus on the pure mechanics of writing, apart from context, blocks the writing process.

If we taught our children to speak in the way that we teach them to write, everyone would stutter.

Mark Twain

Researchers agree that a traditional focus on the pure mechanics of writing can actually harm the natural writing process.

A thorough training in the mechanics of writing does not necessarily produce good writing—and it rarely produces writing from within.

Gabriele Lusser Rico

Neat handwriting, spelling, grammar, and punctuation are drilled at the cost of stifling flowing, imaginative writing. Correct mechanics are important, but are only meaningful when taught in context to children who are already comfortably writing. Writing is no different from learning any other skill. We know as adults that an overload of information and disconnected rules can paralyze us while learning a new skill. Remember your first experiences learning to play a musical instrument or sport. Too much information, which is not yet relevant, is overwhelming. The flow of the activity precedes polishing the skill.

Many teachers believe that children cannot write unless they learn basic skills, which means they expect children to be secretaries before they can become authors.

Frank Smith

Julia Cameron says that there is an important difference between being a good writer and being a good student. She feels that far too many teachers are lint pickers with their red pens. The ultimate obstacle to teaching writing is focusing on handwriting (graphomotor skills) or spelling.

Perfectionism is a primary writer's block.

Julia Cameron

Successful, professional writers let their ideas flow first and later revise mechanical problems. Teaching mechanics first is backwards. Mechanics should be taught within the context of the children's writing. Even at the university level, Wallace Stegner, Stanford professor of creative writing, found that requiring technical writing exercises apart from application in the students' actual works in progress was pointless.

Principle 3

Young writers must first be passionate readers.

Teaching writing involves creating a richly literate environment, a classroom that brims over with books and poetry, storytelling, songs, and people's lives.

Lucy Calkins
The Art of Teaching Writing

Writers **read**. Henry Miller found reading to be as essential to a writer's life as food and exercise. The key to developing young writers is immersion in literature. Nancie Atwell describes herself as someone who "chooses, loves, and lives literature." Her passion is to spark the desire in young people to live truly literate lives. Atwell wants literature to permeate their entire lives, and she models that lifestyle for them.

In her classic text, *In the Middle—Writing, Reading, and Learning with Adolescents*, Atwell describes bringing the dining room table into her classroom. At home, Nancie Atwell, her husband, and friends often sat around the dining room table, discussing books, authors, reading, and writing. They *lived* literature. Atwell successfully brought this concept into the junior high classroom, encouraging students to talk about and live the literature they were reading and writing.

Frank Smith calls this experience "belonging to the writers' or literacy club," apprenticing with other writers and readers. Students must first view themselves as writers. "Reading is the essential source of knowledge about writing," Smith states. Writing teachers agree that reading is the apprenticeship to writing. Immersion in literature in a safe place which encourages open discussion is the foundation for developing writers.

The delight of discovery is a major pleasure of reading; and discovery is one of the best ways to light a fire in a creative mind.
                                                    Wallace Stegner

Writers are our primary teachers; they speak to us from the printed page. Read what you love, and read what challenges and puzzles you. Read works that have lasted over time, and read works that are just appearing in small journals and new anthologies. Read as a writer: How did she surprise me? How did he make me care about that character? Why is this poem line broken as it is? Why doesn't the end of this story work?
                                                    Pat Schneider
                                                    Writing Alone and with Others

Principle 4

The relationship with a writing mentor is the key to effective writing education.

The only way in which anyone learns anything useful about writing is…by personal contact with people, either as individuals or as the authors of books.
                                                    Frank Smith

Frank Smith often asks writers why they started writing. They never mention exercises, grammar lessons, or spelling lists. They all mention a relationship with a writing mentor. Atwell calls this "being hooked by a teacher." She cites many professional authors who were hooked by one teacher.

Having a relationship with a good writing model (teacher, mentor, or parent) is critical to the young author. Researchers agree that students need to see their teachers personally engaged in the activity that they are teaching. Can you imagine studying music with a teacher who did not enjoy making music? Imagine taking painting lessons from an artist who never showed you her paintings or training with a dance coach who never performed. More important than passing on technical skills, arts educators pass on their passion for their art. Writing and literature teachers must pass on the same passion and show students that they are continuing to learn too.

Young writers need feedback and response in a supportive relationship, without judgment. Young authors need "coming alongside" responses *during* the writing process (the draft stage) vs. the traditional, "You finish it, turn it in, and the teacher covers it with red corrections." Developing writers need to apprentice with mentors who are not simply error detectors.

Successful writing teachers bring their own projects in draft stage into the classroom so that students can see their teacher's work in progress and offer suggestions. Children can make insightful contributions. Many children's literature authors ask their own children to critique their stories. Too often students do not understand the writing process because no one has modeled it for them.

Students simply see finished pieces of writing everywhere in their lives, with no understanding of the process the writers went through to reach that final stage. Young writers need to see work in progress to understand that adults struggle with writing too. Problem solving and perseverance are skills learned from their models.

Ideal education is contagious, never forced. Students should see an adult involved in an activity and naturally respond, "I want to learn to do that. Will you teach me?" Young writers need to apprentice with mentors who model a writing lifestyle and openly share their own writing journey, inviting students to join them in the adventure.

Principle 5

Young writers need to be given choices and ownership of their work.

*Finally, I did something I should have known to do long before.
I matched my own reading process against the reading pro-*

*cess I enforced in my classroom. It was not a very close fit. For
example, I usually decide what I'll read, but my students seldom
decided for themselves.*

Nancie Atwell
In the Middle

Children need to be given choices and ownership in their lives. When
deprived of that right, they often feel powerless, angry, and simply stop
caring or participating. That fact was critical in my work as a therapist
with hospitalized children. Patients could not be given a choice about the
medication they received, but they could be given other choices, such
as, "Which arm do you want your IV in? What do you want to play after
your IV treatment? What do you want to eat for lunch today?" Children
with choices become engaged players in their care (or education) instead
of fearful victims.

The more choices we can give young people, the more they will
actively participate in their own learning process. Writing teachers who
incorporate collaborative learning call this "coming out from behind the
desk." Teachers come out from behind the desk, from their position of
unquestionable authority, to learn from students, listen to their input, and
give them choices.

Researchers agree that students must have ownership of what they
write, with the freedom to pick their own writing topics. Not every piece
of writing need be reviewed by a teacher or every journal entry open to
public scrutiny. A student's privacy should be respected. What professional author could comfortably write, knowing that every single piece
he or she wrote would be read by another person, especially judged by an
editor? That would be paralyzing. Writing is a process; to treat each piece
like a finished product blocks the creative flow.

Principle 6

Young writers must be encouraged to bring their personal experiences and struggles—their lives—into their writing.

Real-life authors draw on personal experiences and struggles. They
write because they have no choice. They write out of need, to process

their lives. Denying students this opportunity denies them the power and depth of writing.

We do not write because we want to; we write because we must.

Throw yourself into the hurly-burly of life. It doesn't matter how many mistakes you make, what unhappiness you have to undergo. It is all your material...Don't wait for experience to come to you; go out after experience. Experience is your material.

W. Somerset Maugham

Dr. Rico points out that young children have a natural expressive voice which has disappeared in the university writing students she mentors. "Voice is the authentic sound, rhythm, texture of a unique consciousness on the page...Voice is an expression of the natural you... Finding your own distinctive voice is the actual goal of learning natural writing," she states in *Writing the Natural Way*.

"Writing with voice is writing into which someone has breathed," states Peter Elbow in *Writing with Power*. How can students find their unique voice and style if they are not encouraged to grapple with relevant life issues? "Creative acts most readily arise from the things closest and most profoundly meaningful to us," Rico concludes. Composing a family portrait is a powerful writing assignment in her classes. In leading workshops around the country, Donald Murray found:

I never cease to be surprised at what happens. Even the most private people, those who erect walls between themselves and their associates and neighbors, even their families, start to write of the most personal things: death, loss, disease, pain, driving right to the center of human experience. They write out of need as writers compose out of need.

Write to Learn

Entwining one's life with one's writing is the theme of Lucy Calkin's *Living Between the Lines*. Her students keep life notebooks with them at all times. Calkins agrees that writing to survive is the common thread in authors: "We do not choose writing. It chooses us...Stories can change the world. Stories still push back the darkness and bind us together into communities." She views our lives as stories, and writing as inseparably linked to the life process.

Frank Smith states that "language enables us to put together and express the stories that make our lives meaningful, in whatever culture we live...Language is more powerful than reality." One journalist explains:

When Tara gets upset, she writes—about watching her uncle die of AIDS, about living on the streets of Richmond with friends who stole cars, about her mother leaving her at age 7. And she writes, and cries, of things much worse that she doesn't want to tell anyone. "I feel way down inside and then I start," said the 16-year-old resident of Napa State Hospital. "I think if I didn't write, it would come out in a bad way."

Diana Sugg, *Contra Costa Times*, 10/16/93

Children and adults alike need to make sense of their lives. Writing is life discovery.

Principle 7

Young writers must be read by an audience, published, and treated like working authors.

A book has its origins in the private excitements of the writer's mind. The excitements are private because they're incommunicable unless they're rendered, given extension and resolved as a book.

E. L. Doctorow

Young writers can live the literate lifestyle through open discussion in a safe environment with their peers and models. Most real-life authors write in isolation—they crave that isolation—but they also crave the companionship of other writers and readers. This safe place supports them in their isolated craft. The traditional classroom is often not conducive to isolation nor open discussion for writers.

Students want to share their writing with others and be published.

Writing teachers agree that learning is more likely to occur when students enjoy what they are being asked to do, and when they are grouped to actively learn from each other. The key is that students trust each other, not fearing judgment. Atwell's students keep dialogue journals in which they write letters to her about what they are reading, and she faithfully answers them. Atwell noticed one day that two of her students were writing notes to each other in class about a poem they were studying. She then decided to have students write to one another in their journals to share "literary gossip." Through journaling, students can connect stories they are reading to their own feelings and experiences.

The mark of a great educator, like Nancie Atwell, is the ability to observe what her students are naturally doing and incorporate that into the learning process. Dr. John Hart, a brain researcher, says, "provide the opportunity, stay out of the way, and then observe what the child chooses to do."

After Atwell's seventh grade students moved on to eighth grade, they made the mistake of conferring with each other about their writing in class. Their new teacher was horrified and told them that cheating would not be tolerated. This reminded me of my own daughter's experience after leaving the cooperative learning environment to enter a class where student input and collaboration were no longer welcomed.

Principle 8

The other creative arts, specifically music, should be integrated into the writing program.

The writing of fiction is very sensory. I have to know what a place smells like, what it feels like, and what it sounds like.
Madeleine L'Engle

Writing is an art and should be incorporated with other art forms. This focus strengthens whole-brain learning. Calkins encourages teachers to integrate music whenever possible in the literate environment by setting poetry and stories to music, using rhythm and chants, and celebrating the "song of literature." Children's writing can be set to music too.

Rico believes that writing is too often taught separated from our five senses. Natural writing depends on the multisensory nature of language. We must hear, see, and feel our writing. The rhythmic flow of language, music in words, is a right-brain experience. Voice in writing is authentic sound. Rhythm has been established as a key factor in learning to read and write.

Visual artwork is more often incorporated in the writing program because students enjoy illustrating books they have authored. Music, movement, and dramatization can also be included to heighten the literary experience, ranging from simply listening to music while writing, orchestrating books, or rhythmically setting poems, to producing a full-scale opera written by the class.

While studying the literature of a certain period, students can listen to the music of that same period. Many writers focus more easily when listening to music.

Teachers and parents should be aware that the music education method known as Orff-Schulwerk is an established approach which integrates music, movement, and literature. The composer, Carl Orff (1895–1982), observed that children experience music, movement, and speech (songs, chants) simultaneously in their play, not separately. He believed that children should be taught music as they naturally experience it, through an integration of music, speech, movement, instrumental play, and childhood chants. The term *schulwerk* is the German term for schooling or schoolwork, in this regard in the area of music.

Orff-Schulwerk begins with the child and the creative process, not a desired musical product. Orff believed that rhythm was central to music making and should be developed in early childhood. Orff-Schulwerk is rooted in childhood play, exploration, and creative experience. Orff music teachers include chants, poetry, stories, and dramatic play in music making, evidencing the power of whole-brain learning. Writing mentors should be encouraged to partner with music teachers in exploring the integration of music making, literature, and writing.

Creative people engage in creative activities regularly.
Howard Gardner

Principle 9

Young writers should mentor other student writers.

The most significant part of learning is passing on what we know. Young writers who mentor other students become more expert at their craft. Collaboration with peer writers and the teaching of younger writers is a magical combination of apprenticing in the "writers' club." Atwell shares:

Students who write every day, year in and out, become writers. Something else happens, as well. They become experts at teaching writing. ...They know things I never learned in methods courses or student teaching. They know exactly how and why a writing workshop works. It can get unnerving—some are already such good writing teachers they could put me out of business in a minute.

In the Middle

Principle 10

Young writers need to write every day in environments similar to real-life authors' experiences.

Researchers agree that young writers, like adult authors, need to write daily. Authors will tell you, "The only way to learn to write is...WRITE." Most professional writers observe the discipline of regular writing, agreeing that writing is much more hard work, practice, and perseverance than talent or inspiration ("99% perspiration, 1% inspiration"). Many writers claim *nulla dies sine linea* as their motto: Never a day without a line.

I write every morning even when I don't feel like it. If I stop writing one day, it's going to be harder the next. It's like exercising muscles. If you go for a week without exercising, it's going to ache like crazy when you do. And if you go for a month without exercising, you're going to have lost muscle tone. It's the same thing with writing.

Jane Yolen
How Writers Write

In Summary

The ten principles of effective writing education follow:

1. Learning to write should be a brain-compatible experience.

2. A traditional focus on the pure mechanics of writing, apart from context, blocks the writing process.

3. Young writers must first be passionate readers.

4. A relationship with a writing mentor is the key to an effective writing education.

5. Young writers need to be given choices and ownership of their work.

6. Young writers must be encouraged to bring their personal experiences and struggles—their lives—into their writing.

7. Young writers must be read by an audience, published, and treated like working authors.

8. The other creative arts, specifically music, should be integrated into the writing program.

9. Young writers should mentor other student writers.

10. Young writers need to write every day in environments similar to real-life authors.

This last principle is the focus of our next chapter.

His mother was an illiterate alcoholic.
His grandfather was insane.
He was homely and a loner.
He struggled in school and dropped out at age ten.
His father was a poor shoemaker.
His only comfort was that his father loved him
and read to him every night.
His name was Hans Christian Andersen.

Questions for Reflection

Which principles do you follow with your children?

Which principles do you want to incorporate into your lifestyle?

Who were your significant writing mentors when you were a young person?

The ability to fantasize is the ability to survive.
Creativity is continual surprise.

Ray Bradbury

All good writing is swimming under water
and holding your breath.

F. Scott Fitzgerald

A writer's mind is like flypaper—it traps
whatever happens by.

Richard Selzer

Chapter 5

How Writers Write:
Creating the Writer's Environment

I wake up at 4 a.m., get to my office about 5:15 a.m., work out three times a week, and then I write for about four hours. If I'm not writing, I'm fooling around. But I'm sitting there waiting for God to enter the room.

James McBride

Donald Murray in *Shoptalk* asks the question that I have wondered about for years: Why is the testimony of actual authors about their craft so often ignored by traditional teachers? Often dismissing the professional author as an artist, teachers point out that those experiences are inapplicable to the classroom. That is exactly the educational dilemma.

Think of the many authors, like Faulkner, who were failures in traditional writing classrooms. Beverly Cleary was assigned to the lowest reading group in first grade and regularly feared the teacher's switch. Roald Dahl hated school. His teachers said he was "incapable." Maurice Sendak also detested school. Wilson Rawls, author of *Where the Red Fern Grows*, and Jack London both dropped out of grade school.

Donald Murray, a well-known journalist who later became a university professor of English and an expert in teaching writing to young people, was another struggling student. He explains that he was promoted to junior high school by an elementary school principal who said, "We don't want you around here anymore." Murray doubted that he would finish high school. His refuge became the library where he began collecting quotes by authors about their craft. This was his school. *Shoptalk:*

Learning to Write with Writers is his fascinating compilation of those quotes.

Becoming a Writer

When young people ask me how to get started writing, I tell them the best way would be to go somewhere and do something, experience something, and then write about it.
Richard Rhodes
How to Write: Advice and Reflections

There is no one route to becoming a writer. Let's think of some of our favorite authors of children's literature: Louis Sachar wrote his books while in law school. Frank Baum was a traveling salesman who had failed at everything he attempted in life. Wilson Rawls was a construction worker. Kenneth Grahame was a banker. Grahame wanted to attend college to become a writer but his family called that dream a waste of time. No matter the path they followed, these authors kept writing, apart from traditional training.

Many successful authors trained first in other professions. I recently learned that Tom Clancy writes his novels by inviting military friends to his home to play out various scenarios and see who wins the fictional war. That is certainly collaborative learning at its best. Wouldn't children thrive with such writing games?

A mentor once told me, "Learn everything you can about writing but don't major in the subject in college. Study other fields, live life, or what will you have to write about?" My daughter's journalism professors have advised, "Don't apply to graduate school in journalism. Study the field you intend to write about. Become expert at it so you know what to write."

I am not suggesting that young people should not pursue formal training in writing, yet that is not the main path to becoming a writer.

The Love Affair of Writing

How do real-life authors write? They experience a love affair with creating art through words. Authors' writing habits are as varied as their lives and individual styles. Young writers must have the same freedom.

One moral is that we should never assume that the way we ourselves write is the way everyone writes. Teachers must not assume that their own idiosyncrasies are the only or even the best way to write.

Frank Smith
Writing and the Writer

Researchers and professional writers do agree on one main point: We write to discover what we know. In the actual process of writing, we learn what we think. Flashes of insight and associations emerge that surprise us. One of my favorite quotes, displayed in my office, is:

Dumb writers write what they know. Smart writers write in order to know.

Lewis Smedes

Fiction authors often say that they can't wait to start writing to find out what happens next in their story. The story leads them. The writing takes on a life of its own. Ray Bradbury said, "Find out what your hero or heroine wants, and when he or she wakes up in the morning, just follow him or her all day." Annie Dillard said it a different way, "I do not so much write a book as sit up with it, as with a dying friend."

I have never heard an author say, "Now that I know what I think, I will write it down." Yet isn't this what we ask children to do in the traditional classroom? Donald Murray states: "Schools often teach unnatural, non-writerly attitudes toward writing—know what you want to say before you say it—and students need to see that their own instincts are the instincts of publishing writers." He advises:

Place yourself before a blank piece of paper or a blank computer screen. Do not intend. Wait. Or play around with some words or lines in your daybook or journal, perhaps in a draft. See what happens. Allow words to come; allow language to rearrange

*itself on the page. Perhaps nothing will happen. Don't worry. Try
again another day... Do not fear the emptiness, welcome it, let the
words come at their time in their own order.*

Shoptalk

This approach reinforces whole-brain learning. Researchers agree
that pressuring students, especially with writing tests, only accomplishes
blocking the natural brain processes. I remember as a student receiving
multiple instructions from writing teachers, but I never heard a teacher
say, "Don't worry...relax...see what comes." That is natural writing.
Free-flow writing precedes editing. Editing while pouring one's thoughts
out on paper is pure sabotage. The time for rewriting multiple drafts
comes later.

Nonstop Writing

Write while the heat is in you.

*I put a piece of paper under my pillow and when I could not sleep
I wrote in the dark.*

Henry David Thoreau

Another common habit in authors is that they write **constantly**. They
"write" while they are taking a walk, daydreaming, showering, washing
the dishes, people-watching, doodling on paper, or listening to music.
Poet Jack Prelutsky enjoys writing while in the bathtub. Writing is a lifestyle. No one tells writers when to write. It comes naturally and at odd
times. Many writers work early in the morning or in the middle of the
night. Most authors like to work in complete solitude. A classroom environment filled with distractions would be uncomfortable for them.

Yet other writers, like Donald Murray, tell us that they can write
anywhere that isn't quiet, like a café. The key is ritual. When it is time
to explore their thoughts on paper, if authors block, they get up and walk
around. They get a cup of coffee. Steven Spielberg brainstorms his best
ideas while driving. Stephen King hikes through the woods. Madeleine
L'Engle sits on a chair placed between her desk and piano. When she
needs a break from writing, she simply turns her chair toward the piano
and makes music. Willa Cather read her Bible before writing sessions.

James McBride writes in the morning and works on musical compositions in the afternoon. Jack Prelutsky plays his guitar, setting his poems to music. Many writers are walkers. Robert Frost, Emerson, and Dante composed poetry during their morning walks.

Most of us adults realize that when we block on solving a problem, the quickest way to solve it is to leave the situation and engage in a completely unrelated activity. Then the flash of insight comes and we know the solution. Every author has his or her favorite mindless activity, such as hiking, roller skating, knitting, playing solitaire, or throwing a ball. But these luxuries are rarely afforded to students. We need to remember Bruno Bettelheim's classic statement: "Children know better than adults what they need."

It is sometimes almost as if the problem had to be forgotten to be solved.

Julian Jaynes

Walk-Around Authors

In teaching, you will come to grief as soon as you forget that your pupils have bodies.

Alfred North Whitehead
The Aims of Education, 1929

Nancie Atwell's writers' workshop is filled with places to go. She states, "A reality of adolescence is that junior high students need to move; so do real writers and readers. My students move purposefully among the areas of the room where they find what real writers and readers need."

Authors are serious life observers, gaining ideas from daily events, often the strangest occurrences. Writers are constant jotters. They jot in journals, daybooks, on the backs of envelopes, and other scraps of paper. Writers rarely leave the house without a notebook in hand. They jot throughout the day and night when an idea strikes them. Most writers keep pens and paper by their bed for those 3:00 a.m. insights. You may enjoy browsing through the published notebooks of authors, such as Somserset Maughams' *A Writer's Notebook* or Paula Graham's *Speaking of Journals: Children's Book Writers Talk About their Diaries, Notebooks, and Sketchbooks.*

Velocity is critical to writers. Authors write their first explorations as quickly as possible to insure discoveries and surprises. As Donald Murray states, "Thinking does not precede writing. Writing IS thinking."

Observing how real authors work is the genius behind Lucy Calkins' life notebooks. Students carry them at all times and write when insight strikes. They are given the opportunity to write at all times, whether they are at home, in the park, or in the middle of a science lesson. It is a life process, not to be relegated to an academic structured time slot.

Notebooks can become a habit of life, one that helps us recognize that our lives are filled with material for writing. "Look at the world," notebooks seem to say. "Look at the world in all its grandeur and all its horror. Let it matter."

For this to happen, it is crucial that notebooks leave the four walls of the classroom, and it is also crucial that they be out on children's desks throughout the school day. When writers carry notebooks everywhere, the notebooks nudge us to pay attention to the little moments that normally only flicker into our consciousness.

Lucy Calkins
Living Between the Lines

In Summary

We have observed that working authors have choices about how they work, when they work, and what they write. Their individual habits are respected. They live immersed in the world of literature and writing. They read constantly and write as a lifestyle. Writers apprentice with more skilled authors. They discuss their writing with other writers and pass on their skills to developing writers. This is the chain of companionship and support in the writing craft.

Authors often write first in flowing natural waves of thought—writing what they don't know. They edit the mechanics later. Real-life writers process their personal experiences and struggles through writing. They write to be published and read by an audience. They personally enjoy the creative and imaginative world of the arts.

Every writer enjoys a personal writing ritual which makes him or her comfortable and plays a part in triggering the creative flow of language. We understand the power of association and need to discover what makes young writers comfortable; it will be different for each. Maybe one student needs to find an isolated, quiet corner, another needs to take a walk, another might be helped by listening to music, while another may need to brainstorm with other students. Our individual temperaments and learning styles play a part in our writing rituals. Students will have different times of the day which are peak times for writing.

This flexibility may sound unrealistic but it evidences another place where the traditional classroom structure collides with how the natural creative brain process flows. No wonder Frank Smith said, "Schools are not good places in which to learn to write and read." **Yet the home can be the ideal haven for creating an environment where young writers can flourish.**

One of my favorite music professors in graduate school, upon entering class, would give us mathematical or logic puzzles to solve before beginning his lectures. At first we thought he was a little crazy. These puzzles had nothing to do with music history, but everything to do with education. Many of us were teachers. As we would block on solving a puzzle, he would encourage, "Think outside the box. See it in a new way, a way you've never looked at it before. Don't settle for doing things the way you've always done them."

Even today, when my husband and I face a problem that appears unsolvable, we stop and remember, "We've got to think outside the box." There is always a creative solution.

Effective writing mentors listen to their students and find new solutions to old problems, seeking out new opportunities to inspire young authors.

Young writers prove that thinking outside the box is far easier for children than adults. Our challenge is to learn from them.

My work habits are simple: long periods of thinking, short periods of writing.

Ernest Hemingway

Questions for Reflection

Which writing habits or rituals do you share with real-life authors?

Children do not always listen to their parents, but they never fail to imitate them.

James Baldwin

Train up a child in the way he should go—and walk there yourself once in a while.

Josh Billings

When a family reads a book together, the people in the book become family friends.

Mary Pipher

Chapter 6

The Parent's Role
as Writing Mentor

Example is the school of mankind, and they will learn at no other.
Edmund Burke

If you only remember one statement from this book, let this be it: **As a parent, you are your child's most influential writing mentor. You are the example.** If you are passionate about writing, your child will probably learn to love writing. If you detest writing, your child may mirror your attitude.

You may be familiar with Anthony Trollope's novels but you may not have heard about his mother. She rose at 4:00 every morning and wrote to support her family. She had four children (two were chronically ill) and a sick husband. She nursed a son, daughter, and husband to their deaths and never stopped writing. She encouraged her son, Anthony, in his desire to write and helped him find his first publisher. Anthony Trollope's mother was his primary model.

Dr. Ben Carson, director of pediatric neurosurgery at Johns Hopkins Hospital, credits his mother as his inspiration. She was one of 24 children, never attended school beyond the third grade, and was married by age thirteen. She was illiterate but insisted that her son value education and the written word.

Whether you homeschool your child, partner with your child's classroom teacher and augment with activities at home, or lead a writing group with your family or other children, you cannot escape the fact that you are your child's most important model. Your job is to create an environment conducive to writing in the home. Suzuki music education is one of the most effective brain-compatible methods used today. Developing the parent as home teacher is critical to the approach. Let us study this model as an example before applying the concepts to writing education.

Suzuki Talent Education

Character first, ability second.
Shinichi Suzuki

Shinichi Suzuki developed his method in Japan while working with exceptional children and youth who had been traumatized during World War II. His primary goal was to use music to bring healing to young people. He believed that a musical life was an enriched and joyful life.

Dr. Suzuki's work is founded on the mother tongue concept. He observed that all children learn to speak their native tongue with great mastery due to immersion in language sounds from birth. He spent his life's work demonstrating that similar immersion in a musical home environment develops an equally remarkable ability in music. What opportunities exist in the environment will naturally develop traits in the child. At the Talent Education School in Matsumoto, Suzuki's philosophy extends beyond musical training, and other abilities are nurtured using the same method.

The ability development, or talent education, method refers to Suzuki's belief that talent is a myth. Any child can develop an ability or talent if provided with the proper environment in which the stimulus is repeated often enough. He values the human potential of any individual and believes that there are no failures. Though it is never too late to begin the Suzuki process, the method is rooted in starting children from birth. Children are exposed daily to high quality music recordings in their environment. Models who make beautiful music are crucial.

Children begin formal music instruction in the preschool years and continue the process as a way of life. Regular practice throughout the day is encouraged. Suzuki advocates emphasize that it is not a music education method but a lifestyle.

Suzuki music making is a product of listening and experience, not matching notes on a page. He believes that teaching a child to read music before he can make music is analogous to teaching a child to read before he can speak. Symbols cannot be associated with a process that one has never experienced. Music reading is postponed until after the child's music skills are comfortably established.

The Suzuki method focuses on the total well-being and self-esteem of children, not their musical product. Learning blocks can occur as the result of criticism or pressure. The Suzuki teacher provides a safe and joyful learning environment where the student is always affirmed. The Suzuki program is a group experience. Students have private sessions with their teachers and also attend group classes to make music with others. An attitude of cooperation (vs. competition) and helping one another is fostered.

The Suzuki method is a family method. The parent is the home teacher. The parent attends all lessons, takes notes, and receives instruction. If not already a musician, the parent will become one. The parent works with the child daily at home. The teacher, student, and parent form the "Suzuki triangle." Without the cooperation of parents and partnership with the home, the Suzuki method cannot succeed.

Where love is deep, much can be accomplished.
Shinichi Suzuki

Any work of art is the product of a total human being.
Wallace Stegner

Writing as Arts Education

Now let's compare the ten principles for creating a writer's environment covered in Chapter Four with the Suzuki method. Both approaches:

—teach children in the way their brains naturally process.

—immerse children in a richly literate or musical environment, based on the belief that talent is a myth.

—give children high-quality models through literature or recordings, and through contact with real-life writers or musicians.

—teach mechanics after the ability has been comfortably acquired.

—are about a lifestyle vs. a separate subject area.

—focus on the process of developing esteem and wholeness in children vs. a product.

—offer avenues for publication or performance to reach an audience.

—provide group sessions to share and celebrate one's art with peers in a safe environment.

—are based on regular practice throughout the day as a natural lifestyle.

—use teachers and parents as supportive mentors vs. critical error-detectors.

—share the goal of passing on the joy and passion of music making or writing for life.

Another Approach: Charlotte Mason's Methods

Charlotte Mason's classic approach is similar to the Suzuki method and remains popular with home schooling famies. Mason's philosophy is based on immersing children in high quality literature ("living books" that engage a child) and art work. She believed that young people learn from being exposed to the best original works in our culture, not from watered down textbook versions.

She encouraged students to keep journals and nature notebooks, safe places to draw and write about their life experiences. She advocated going on nature walks to explore our world firsthand. Instead of correcting a child's piece of writing with a red pen ("error detecting"), Mason asked students to copy passages from literature, modeling excellent writing for them. She felt this method was a more positive way to teach grammar, spelling, and writing techniques. In addition, students kept notebooks for creating historical time lines, practicing spelling and dictation, and narrating or "telling back" what they recently learned.

Mason's goal was to inspire a lifetime passion for learning in students. She founded her interactive methods on the Latin word for education, "educare," meaning to feed and nourish. Mason viewed learning as a lifestyle.

Mason encouraged children to keep copywork notebooks to provide ongoing practice for handwriting, spelling, grammar, etc. Copywork teaches accuracy and attention to detail, and students discover things about the text they are copying that they would be unlikely to notice otherwise. Students learn correct spelling, capitalization, punctuation, and other language mechanics when they compare their work to the original and correct their mistakes. In the back of this book is a month of writing quotes that can be used for copywork.

The Parent's Role

If your son cannot be a future major league ball player, should he join a baseball team? If your daughter is not going to be a concert pianist, should she study music? If your child cannot be a future Tolstoy or Shakespeare, should he or she be encouraged to write? Should your investment in your child's well-being or skills be based on how much he or she will contribute to society? These questions may sound ridiculous, but there is a subtle undercurrent in our society which measures our children's success by their visible accomplishments.

This book was no more written to turn out professional writers than I teach music to students with special needs to develop concertizing musicians. While many piano students dread their weekly lessons, my students enjoy making music in the here and now. They do not endure lessons for a future payoff. Education must be relevant today.

What are practical ways that parents can become writing mentors and put these principles into practice? We may be working with our child's classroom teacher to create a "writing triangle" or we may be our child's primary writing mentor. We may be developing a writing group at home. Our task as parents remains the same: to develop an environment which fosters writing.

Power struggles are pointless. Nagging children about practicing or finishing homework writing exercises can do more damage than good; yet by taking them to a concert, listening to an exceptional recording, or reading a fascinating book, you will inspire your children without saying a word.

The mark of a good Suzuki teacher is the ability to show, not tell. This principle applies to all aspects of effective education.

We are our children's first writing models.

Our children need to see us **write**. The old adage "children will do what you do, not what you say" is never more true than in education. We need to model the writing process, showing our children our own work in progress, whether it is a letter to a friend, a recent journal entry, or a business plan. We show them that writing is relevant and useful in life. When we journal, our children observe the power of processing life through writing. When we attend writing groups, our children observe that writing can be shared with others. Some working authors encourage their children to help proofread and edit their writing projects, involving them in the process.

We as adults can improve our own writing in order to model learning for our children. Excellent resources are *On Writing Well* by William Zinsser and *The Writer's Art* by James Kilpatrick. Classic texts for honing writing skills are *The Elements of Style* by Strunk and White, and *Woe is I* by Patricia O'Connor.

We can become better readers by reading *How to Read a Book* by Mortimer Adler. We can become familiar with research about the child's writing process, reading the same books that writing teachers read.

We are our children's first research assistants when they are writing nonfiction projects. We help them find references, show them how to write letters to obtain information from organizations or resource experts, or assist them in setting up interviews. We can guide them in tapping available resources. My children actually help me with computer searches.

Lucy Calkins says that absorption and fascination with a subject are what matter most in nonfiction research: "…I know the challenge of writing nonfiction has everything to do with the fact that when a person cares deeply about a subject, that caring draws not only the writer but also the reader into a living relationship with that subject." We as parents must become excited and care as deeply as our children do about the topic they are researching.

My son was recently asked to write a report on ALS (amyotrophic lateral sclerosis). His science teacher required the students to not only research the facts about a disease but interview a person who lived with the disease. As my son and I sat with the family who had graciously allowed my son to interview them, I observed my son's reaction as he realized that a disease had actual human faces and suffering souls.

I am always amazed at the number of people I meet—well-educated people—who cannot remember the last book they read, or who rarely write. They quickly offer, "I hate to write." It is as if the minute they left school, they were glad to be free of those constraints. When teachers fail to ignite a lifelong passion, or at least a use, for the subject they teach, then they have ultimately failed. Our challenge today is that parents who were taught in traditional classroom writing environments often have no love for writing. Igniting a joy for writing in adults is the key.

We have the responsibility to create a richly literate home environment.

The gift of creative reading, like all natural gifts, must be nourished or it will atrophy. And you nourish it, in much the same way you nourish the gift of writing—you read, think, talk, look, listen, hate, fear, love, weep—and bring all of your life like a sieve to what you read. That which is not worthy of your gift will quickly pass through, but the gold remains.

Katherine Paterson
A Sense of Wonder

I love to enter a home and see books everywhere. Parents are also their child's first reading model. Some children have never seen their parents absorbed in a book. How can they be excited about reading? We must immerse our children in the world of literature. Through excursions to libraries, poetry readings, or the theater to attend plays, we communicate the value of literature. We can search for opportunities to see real-life authors in action when we attend book signings by visiting authors at local bookstores.

Wallace Stegner may not be a Suzuki teacher but he states, "Those who hear a lot of poetry in their youth are likelier to become poets than those who do not."

We need to be knowledgeable about high-quality literature and invest in creating a home library. We should read with our children—to them as well as beside them. There is nothing as magical as spending a rainy evening by the fireplace with members of the family each absorbed in their own books. We share the companionship of reading. Children are never too old to be read to; it is a relationship of discovery together.

Books are a priority in the literate home. Not only books, but the time to read them is made a priority. When our children were young, our ritual was to visit the library weekly, bringing home armfuls of books, and spend two hours every morning reading. My children always awakened early so we made hot chocolate and read from about 7:00 to 9:00 a.m. daily. The phone didn't ring. No one knocked on the door. Our time was completely uninterrupted. I learned then to always do the most important thing first before the chaos of the day began.

We as a family have enjoyed becoming immersed in authors. We encouraged our children to become "author experts." One of our daughters became fascinated with Roald Dahl. She read every one of his books, including his cookbook and autobiography. She observed how each incidence in his autobiography became the basis for one of his stories. She became a "Roald Dahl expert." She then planned to write to him and was upset to learn that he was deceased. My son wrote to his favorite author through his publishing company in England. We doubted that we would ever hear from the author, but months later, a wonderful letter arrived for my son, answering his questions.

We can help our children find the biographies of their favorite authors in order to understand their lives, such as Roald Dahl's *Boy*, or Beverly Cleary's *A Girl From Yamhill*. Your local librarian can assist you. Also look for wonderful collections of stories and authors' life anecdotes, such as Jim Trelease's *Hey! Listen to This, Stories to Read Aloud*. Pamela

Lloyd's *How Writers Write* is an excellent compilation of children's authors' descriptions of their writing processes.

We can become literary partners with our children, no matter their ages. As they become older, we can keep dialogue journals, similar to Nancie Atwell's process, to correspond about current reading. Even in high school literature classes, I remember that my mother read my assigned books to be able to discuss them with me. Effective literacy and writing are family affairs.

Literate families are informal book clubs. Often a good book makes the rounds through our extended family, making meaningful discussions possible between our children and other family members. Weaving reading into a natural lifestyle is more effective than academic assignments.

> *Who would call a day spent reading a good day?*
> *But a life spent reading—that is a good life.*
> Annie Dillard
> *The Writing Life*

We can celebrate life with books and writing.

We human beings are in charge of celebration.
Byrd Baylor

Children crave celebration. We can connect the world of literature and writing with childhood joy. Books are wonderful gifts to celebrate a job well done, a good report card, or an upcoming trip. We can celebrate authors' birthdays, weave writing into holiday celebrations, and include writing games in family dinner activities. More ideas will follow in Section Six.

Children are never too young to start "writing." The beginning is storytelling. Drawing pictures follows and written language eventually emerges. The process of writing starts years before children are able to make letters, just as music making starts years before notes can be read on a page. Younger siblings can be fully included in writing celebrations. Older siblings can serve as mentors. Cooperative learning begins in the home. As much as I believe this, I was still surprised when our three-year-old son asked to be taken to the store to buy his own "writers' workshop journal like Sissy's." He enjoyed writing letters to grandparents, drawing pictures, and telling stories.

We must cultivate our children's imaginations.

Excursions of the imagination are often considered to be a waste of time, distraction, escapes from reality—irresponsible even. Fantasizing, daydreaming, and talking to ourselves may be regarded as indulgent if not reprehensible private activities. But imagining is something else that the brain does continually. Far from being an escape from reality, imagination makes reality possible.

Frank Smith
to think

One of the most important gifts we can give our children is the time and freedom to allow their imaginations to run wild. We know that play is the child's work. Home should be the safe retreat of the imagination. Children need to daydream. We observed that real-life authors "write" as they daydream and play in the world of imagination. E. B. White, C. S. Lewis, and Kenneth Grahame hid in attic retreats as children to daydream. Children today need the same opportunity.

In our achievement-oriented society, it is difficult for parents to allow children this freedom. We come upon a child lying in bed, staring at the ceiling, when he is supposed to be cleaning his room or finishing his homework. Our first response is, "Stop fooling around. You have work to do." Obviously there is a balance but most tired parents err on the side of getting the job done vs. cultivating their child's imagination. When author Dr. Louise DeSalvo wrote as a child, her parents told her to "get busy on her homework and chores."

Parents need to protect children from becoming involved in too many activities, so they have time to develop their imaginations. Today some children with nonstop lifestyles and "stressaholic" patterns often do not know what to do when they are presented with free time, apart from watching television or playing video games.

Children are unusually receptive to imagery. Storytelling begins in the imagination. Many authors, such as Frances Hodgson Burnett, C. S. Lewis, Sue Alexander, Joan Aiken, and Rumer Godden, began their writing careers as children telling stories to their friends and siblings. The author/illustrator, Steven Kellogg, "told stories on paper" to his sister. Those stories which held young listeners spellbound later became published books.

Schools are traditionally not places where children are allowed to daydream and live in the world of imagination. The home must certainly be that safe place.

Most people dismiss most of their imaginative life with amused indifference, and maybe even a little contempt. This is where you (as a writer) must part company with most people. Your fantasies are a resource, and the place where they change and mingle in your mind is the place where ideas are conceived.
                     Stephen Koch
                     The Modern Library Writer's Workshop

We as parents must not pigeonhole our children's literary gifts.

Parents must recognize that children successfully write in different ways. Children develop a writing lifestyle which suits their uniquely wired brains.

Our oldest daughter, Janelle, identifies herself as a writer. Her favorite classes throughout school have been English literature and journalism courses. Our younger daughter, Natalie, identifies herself as a scientist, mathematician, musician—anything but a writer. She claims to hate writing, yet I have observed that she hates academic writing. Far more than her older sister, Natalie uses writing constantly in real life. When we are traveling on vacation, she writes in her journal daily and writes lengthy letters to her friends. She talks to them on paper. When she is concerned about friends, she writes them heartfelt letters. She creates involved planning notebooks for coming events. Written communication is a natural part of her life.

We must not stereotype our children's approach to writing. Academic writing is only one form of writing.

Our families can use writing
to process life and problem-solve.

We construct stories to make sense of events.
Language permits the imagination and emotions to flourish.
Language is more powerful than reality.

Frank Smith

Beyond writing education, parents need to be aware of the importance of writing and literature as coping tools in life. Calkins uses life notebooks as an extension of the classroom into real life, where students can freely write about their struggles, such as coping with illness, death, anger, and loneliness, as they read books touching similar topics.

Bibliotherapy, therapeutic storytelling, creative writing, and journaling are powerful methods for coping with crises. Having integrated the use of books and writing often in my work as a creative arts therapist with hospitalized children, I integrate them in our home as well. When we give children the gift of processing their lives through writing, reading, and the arts, we give them a lifetime tool for coping and problem solving.

Therapeutic journaling is a powerful tool in interpreting reality and adapting to crisis. Two excellent resources are *Pain and Possibility: Writing Your Way Through Personal Crisis* by Gabriele Rico and *Writing as a Way of Healing* by Dr. Louise DeSalvo.

Writing out of pain is not a unique occurrence. Many authors survived tragic childhoods. Nathaniel Hawthorne, Beatrix Potter, and Anna Sewell were invalids. Confined to bed, they created their own worlds. Anna Sewell, author of *Black Beauty*, never rode a horse. Kenneth Grahame, Frances Hodgson Burnett, C. S. Lewis, Roald Dahl, and Eric

Knight as children each lost parents to death and then endured sudden poverty. Pain is the thread in many of our favorite classic stories. In each childhood, there existed one person who read to the young writers, loved them, and gave them the gift of literature.

Walt and Roy Disney built a new home for their parents after the success of *Snow White and the Seven Dwarfs©*. A defective furnace left their mother dead and their father widowed. Many of the subsequent Disney© animated stories had themes of loss and deceased parents.

Novelist Nicholas Delbanco once said that by age four one has experienced nearly everything one needs as a writer of fiction: love, pain, loss, boredom, rage, guilt, and fear of death.

Anyone who survived childhood has enough material to write for the rest of his or her life.
                                                            Flannery O'Connor

In Summary

Summarizing the preceding principles, parents:

—are their children's first writing models.

—have the responsibility to create a richly literate home environment.

—can celebrate life with books and writing.

—must cultivate their children's imaginations.

—must not pigeonhole their children's literary gifts.

—can use writing to process life and solve problems.

When they can choose, junior high students will write for all the reasons literate people everywhere engage as writers: to re-create happy times, work through sad times, discover what they know about a subject and learn more, convey and request information, apply for jobs, parody, petition, play, argue, apologize, advise, make money. When they can choose, students will read for all the reasons literate people everywhere engage as readers: to live other lives and learn about their own, to see how other writers have written and to acquire other writers' knowledge, to escape, think, travel, ponder, laugh, cry.

Nancie Atwell
In the Middle

Questions for Reflection

Did your parents mentor you as a writer? What examples did they set?

How do you mentor your children?

A professional writer is an amateur who didn't quit.
Richard Bach

Showing up is the main thing.

Jack Heffron

But if I write what my soul thinks, it will be visible, and the words will be its body.

Helen Keller

If you are a writer, you locate yourself behind a wall of silence and no matter what you are doing, driving a car or walking or doing housework, which I love, you can still be writing, because you have that space.

Joyce Carol Oates

Chapter 7

Parent to Parent:
Three Major Myths About the Writing Life

If you want to write, finally you'll find a way no matter what.
Natalie Goldberg

If you purchased this book, there is a good chance that you already have a passion for the written word. Perhaps writing is your avocation, your lifeline through the challenges of life. Or you may be a professional writer. Professionalism in our culture has become synonymous with receiving monetary compensation for a skill, but that is not the original definition of the word.

A professional is defined as one who is engaged in a calling requiring specialized knowledge and preparation - a principal calling, vocation, or employment.

You may consider yourself a professional writer, whether you receive compensation or not. I learned that fact from some ten-year-olds. Your true compensation may far exceed what a publisher's contract can offer you…sanity, and an enriched and creative life.

If you are reading this book, however, there is a greater chance that you have a family who constantly interrupts your days and derails your best-laid plans. Did you know that this is your greatest asset as a writer? Living fully is critical to good writing. Katherine Paterson said it best:

…success might have come sooner if I'd had a room of my own and fewer children, but I doubt it. For as I look at my writing, it seems to me that the very persons who take away my time and space are the ones who have given me something to say.
Gates of Excellence

Pursuing your own passion for writing is the single best way to encourage your children to write. Perhaps you have not taken this path because you have believed three major myths about the writing lifestyle:

Myth #1: Writing requires more time than I have.

Myth #2: Writing requires an isolated lifestyle without interruptions.

Myth #3: It's too late in life for me to become a writer.

Both young and adult writers need to realize that these statements are myths. Parents who want to write should know that a lack of concentrated time has never stopped anyone from pursuing this craft who was passionate about writing. Here are some examples:

—Toni Morrison was a single parent who worked full-time as an editor to support her family. She said that she wrote around the edges of her day. She published *Beloved* in her fifties.

—William Faulkner wrote *As I Lay Dying* in six weeks, in spare moments during a twelve-hour-a-day manual labor job. Later he worked as a postman, but he was not a very good postman. He would throw away letters he didn't want to deliver.

—Poet Audre Lorde scribbled poems while waiting in supermarket check-out lines.

—Ann Tyler was a busy mom who made notes for book projects during her daughter's slumber parties.

—Marcel Proust wrote *Remembrance of Things Past* in the middle of the night, as he lay in bed suffering with asthma.

—Flannery O'Connor wrote some of her best works while she was dying with lupus.

—Scott Turow wrote his first novel while riding the daily commuter train to and from his law office.

—Though Stephen King had a college degree in English and teaching credentials, he worked in a laundry, writing at lunch and after work.

—D. H. Lawrence wrote poetry while sitting by the bedside of his dying mother.

—Successful novelist Nancy Peacock continues to clean houses for a living because she can work while brainstorming about her writing.

Myth #1: A Lack of Time

One of the biggest myths around writing is that in order to do it we must have great swathes of uninterrupted time.

Julia Cameron
The Right to Write

Most writers agree that we do not find the time to write; we steal those moments whenever we can. I have written while sitting on park benches, in cars, in doctors' offices, and in a host of unusual places while waiting for my children. I have written on the kitchen counter while cooking dinner. When we writers are not actually putting pen to paper or sitting at our computers, we are usually engaged in thinking about our writing (called "musing" by some writers) or reading works by other writers. These three activities dovetail.

Myth #2: Needed Isolation

...Albert Facey wrote A Fortunate Life *on one end of the kitchen table while his wife peeled vegetables on the other...*

Patti Miller
Writing Your Life

Writers agree that isolating ourselves to write often starves us of input. We need to be in the mainstream of life. Wallace Stegner describes writers as those "on whom nothing is lost." We do not go out seeking experiences to write about. We simply recognize their value when they occur in our lives and want to share them with others.

Julia Cameron explains in *The Right to Write*:

When we center our writing lives on our writing instead of on our lives, we leach both our lives and our writing of the nutrients they require.

Instead of viewing the people in our lives and the dilemmas, interruptions, and challenges we face as obstacles to our writing, we can view them as rich, necessary material. They are the ones who have given us something to say.

In Charles Dickens' era, daughters were sent to boarding schools while sons of poor families entered the work force. While Dickens' sister, Fanny, was sent to the Royal Academy, 12-year-old Charles was required to stop schooling to work ten hours a day in a factory. When their father was sentenced to debtors' prison, Fanny remained in boarding school while Charles worked. His life experiences were the inspiration for many of his novels.

Myth #3: It's Too Late

It's never too late in life to learn a new skill or pursue a new life adventure. Many of our favorite novels were written by those in their midlife or later years. Harriet Beecher Stowe published *Uncle Tom's Cabin* in her forties. George Eliot published *Middlemarche* in her fifties.

As a baby, James Michener was abandoned on a widow's doorstep. He was in and out of orphanage care. Caring people read to him. He wrote his first book when he was forty years old and then published forty-eight books in the second half of his life.

Writers bring a wealth of experience to their craft. There is no substitute for life experience. Dismiss any myths you may hold about the writing life. When you weave writing into your lifestyle, you inspire your children to do the same. You are their strongest influence.

I got so discouraged, I almost stopped writing. It was my 12-year-old son who changed my mind when he said to me, "Mother,

you've been very cross and edgy with us and we notice you
haven't been writing. We wish you'd go back to the typewriter."...
At that point, I acknowledged that I am a writer and even if I
were never published again, that's what I am.

Madeleine L'Engle
in *Shoptalk* by Donald Murray

Questions for Reflection

Have you believed any of these myths?

Do you view yourself as a writer?

How have the people and interruptions in your life given you
something to say?

No human being is so poor as to have no trace of genius.
Shinichi Suzuki

It is well to understand as early as possible in one's writing life that there is just one contribution which every one of us can make: we can give into the common pool of experience some comprehension of the world as it looks to each of us. There is one sense in which everyone is unique.
Dorothea Brande

If you are writing the clearest, truest words you can find and doing the best you can to understand and communicate, this will shine on paper like its own lighthouse. Lighthouses don't go running all over an island looking for boats to save; they just stand there shining.
Anne Lamott

Section III

Publishing Process
for the Writing Group

Chapter 8

Beginning the Publishing Process

You don't write because you want to say something; you write because you have something to say.

F. Scott Fitzgerald

The definition of "publish" is to make public. Writers, young and old, want to share their work and be published. Since relevancy and application to current life are the keys to effective education, immersion in the world of real-life authors was an important part of my daughter's writing group program. In addition to working on their own writing projects, the children sometimes took field trips to visit authors they respected. Upon returning, they then wrote letters to their favorite authors, thanking them for their time.

One afternoon, Mrs. Thomas invited me to come and answer questions about the publishing process. "Do you make lots of money?" and "Will we make lots of money writing books?" were the children's first questions. "No," I answered, "many writers do not make lots of money. Most writers will tell you that they simply *have* to write. It is not really a choice. Ideas consume them until they can express them on paper. Authors usually write for the love of writing, not money."

"How do you think an author's work becomes published?" I asked the children. "You just sit down and write a book. Then someone publishes it," they were quick to reply, disappointed that they would not be independently wealthy soon. Their second disappointment was that I wrote boring adult nonfiction books, not colorful picture books or fantasy stories.

I explained the steps in the publishing process, showing the young writers examples of query letters, proposals, contracts, manuscripts, galleys, cover samples, and promotional ads. They had no idea that bringing a book to print was such an involved process. Then I asked the children to list the qualities of a good writer. They brainstormed and came up with the following:

"You must have good ideas."

"You have to know how to write well."

"You must have patience."

"You need to read a lot."

"You probably need computer skills."

"You should do your own research."

"You must have perseverance."

"You should learn and experience different things in life to able to write about them."

We agreed that all these qualities were important in a writer. Then I asked them, "Do you want to go through a realistic publishing process this year? Do you want to be treated as real-life authors?" The young writers discussed the pros and cons among themselves and unanimously voted to participate.

We discussed various genres of literature they enjoyed reading and might be interested in exploring as writers. They listed these:

Autobiographies

Biographies

Fairy tales and modernized fairy tales

Fiction

Historical fiction

Illustrated children's books

Memoirs

Nonfiction

Plays/Musicals

Poetry

As the young writers brainstormed together, they each began to refine an idea into a potential book project. I explained that authors first contact different publishers to see if they are interested in their book ideas. The children were surprised to learn that authors do not simply send a completed book to a publisher.

During the following weeks, we began working through the steps to become published. The first two steps we covered were writing a query letter and developing the proposal.

Step #1: The Query Letter

The children learned to write a query letter, explaining their potential book project. They each designed their own letterhead and wrote a one-page formal business letter to the fictional publisher, Creative Concepts Publications. The young writers briefly described their book ideas and offered their qualifications to write the book. They addressed the envelopes to a fictional address and gave them to their teacher to "mail."

Step #2: The Proposal

A letter from Creative Concepts Publications was waiting for each child at their next group meeting, asking them to submit a proposal. Proposal guidelines were included in each envelope. The children were excited that the publisher was interested in their ideas and eagerly set to work on writing their proposals, a project that would span two months. These are the guidelines they received:

Creative Concepts Publications
Proposal Guidelines

Please submit to us:
- Cover Letter
    Write a brief business letter introducing the proposal.
- Book Title
- Table of Contents
    An outline or mindmap may be substituted.

- Sample Chapter
- Author's Background
  Explain why you are qualified to write this book.
- Market Overview

Answer these questions: Are other books written on this topic? What are related books? Do you see a need for your book? Why is your book unique? Who is your audience?

The young writers tackled a different part of the proposal each week as they continued working on their stories.

The Mutiny

Then we experienced the beginnings of a mutiny. "We just want to write... not work on these assignments," the children told us. Always taking our cue from the children, Mrs. Thomas and I put the proposal project on the shelf and encouraged the children to simply write without restrictions, fall in love with their stories, and enjoy the magic of creating them. We wouldn't interfere.

One young girl was writing a modernized version of *Jack and the Beanstalk*. One young man was exploring the trauma his family experienced when his dog was injured and confined to a dog wheelchair during the same period that his father had a heart attack. My daughter and her friend were collaborating on a sequel to one of their favorite books, *The Phantom Tollbooth*. Another young author was writing a play to be performed by the writing group. Another young man went home after the first session and wrote his entire book in one week, a tale of historical fiction called *Lost at Sea*. He saw little need for the proposal, a feeling shared by many authors when their books are already completed. Few professional authors enjoy the business side of selling a book.

Proposal Revisited

Once the children were immersed in writing again and had completed their stories, they were interested in sending chapters to the publisher.

They wanted to finish the proposals and began working on their resumés as writers. They included in their author's background section:

—their academic career at their elementary school and unique accomplishments.

—their special interests and hobbies.

—previous books that they had published in their third grade writers' workshop.

The young writers spent their next group session sitting at computers at the public library, searching for books that were similar to their stories. Was their book idea original or had it already been published? Who would want to read their book? The children were determined to convince the publisher that there was a need for their books. They had not wanted to complete this research before writing their stories. Many wonderful books have been written by authors with the same creative blinders on. Writers must believe in their projects, not becoming discouraged before they start.

Completing the Proposal

The proposals were now complete and ready to send to Creative Concepts Publications. The children wrote cover letters and assembled their information according to the proposal guidelines. They put the proposals in large manila envelopes, addressed them to the publisher, and gave them to their teacher to mail. I explained that the proposals would now be either accepted or rejected. I told the children that proposals were rarely accepted by the first contacted publisher; real-life authors contact several publishers before finding the right match for their book ideas.

There was some confusion about whether the proposals were being sent to a real publisher. I had always told the writing group that this was a fictional process, but perhaps now it had become too real. These children had invested so much of themselves. I became nervous.

Similar to any major project, the proposal process bogged down toward the end. Often the closer we writers come to the finish line, the harder it can be to keep on pushing. Yet Mrs. Thomas knew what to do. She told the writing group that if their proposals were completed by the third week in December, she would host a Christmas tree decorating party at her home, complete with making gingerbread houses and Christmas cookies. Every proposal was completed by the deadline, and not one young writer missed the party. She asked the children if they wanted to include their families in the proposal celebration. They unanimously answered, "No! We are the ones who worked hard. This party is only for us." The group's identity was unshakable. They alone had shared this experience; all others were outsiders.

I marveled at Mrs. Thomas' gift for motivating children. I was working on my own major project at the time, editing a college textbook with twenty other contributors from around the country. Being busy professionals, many of the contributors had not yet sent their chapters and were months past deadline. Would a tree-decorating party work for them?... Tickets to Hawaii? A Caribbean cruise?

Everyone needs tangible and pleasurable incentives in life. The gift is knowing what incentives will work...and having the checkbook to support them.

There is no such thing as writer's block. My father drove a truck for 40 years. And never once did he wake up in the morning and say: "I have truck driver's block today. I am not going to work."

Roger Simon

Questions for Reflection

What do you think are the necessary qualities of a good writer?

What are the qualities of a writer who can bring a completed work to publication?

Do the qualities differ?

Writing is the hardest way to make a living, with the possible exception of wrestling alligators.
Olen Miller

If you are willing to fail, you can also fly.
Karen Propp

It is better to fail in originality, than to succeed in imitation.
Herman Melville

Chapter 9

Rejection Day

Better to write for yourself and have no public, than write for the public and have no self.

Cyril Connolly

Don't ask me why, but I decided that leading the children through a realistic publishing process required the experience of rejection. Rejection slips are an unavoidable part of the writer's life. Stephen King nailed them to the wall above his writing desk. Other well-known authors have their own collections.

Books by the finest writers are rejected by publishers. In hindsight, I wonder why I thought that nine- and ten-year-old children were tough enough to face an experience that could reduce many writers to tears on a bad day. I no longer thought of them as children but as young professional writers, hoping to encourage them to never quit.

At our next session, I handed out the rejection letters from Creative Concepts Publications. I asked the children to not speak to one another after opening the letters and write down how they were feeling. When I witnessed the anger on their faces, I feared that I had pushed the authentic publishing experience too far. The children were furious and felt betrayed. They each wrote variations on the theme "I AM SO ANGRY" in giant lettering. The young writers read their written feelings to the group, as their fellow authors cheered them on. Had I destroyed their spirits?

Quit or Fight?

I told these developing writers that they had a critical decision to make. They could give up on their projects or they could fight for their book ideas, no matter what the publisher thought. "Oh, forget it…it's not worth it…let's just give up…," they echoed each other. Then I asked them if they thought that some of their favorite authors had experienced rejection. "Of course not," they replied. Then our discussion began. I asked them, "Did you know that…?"

—Dr. Seuss' first book was rejected more than thirty times.

—E. B. White's book, *Stuart Little*, met with rejection for seven years. The children's librarian emeritus of the New York Public Library wrote that the book would be damaging to children and the project should be immediately abandoned.

—William Faulkner, winner of the Nobel Prize in literature, flunked his first English course and dropped out of college, misunderstood by his professor. Leo Tolstoy also flunked out of college and was described as unable and unwilling to learn.

—Frank Baum's *Oz* series was disliked by librarians and teachers. They said his books lacked literary merit and his genre of fantasy was inappropriate for children.

—John Steinbeck's *Grapes of Wrath* was described as a failure and a disappointing melodrama by one critic.

—Herman Melville's *Moby Dick* and James Joyce's *Ulysses* were described by reviewers as "midden"—a dunghill, a pile of trash.

—Margaret Mitchell's *Gone with the Wind* was rejected by more than 25 publishers.

—Beatrix Potter's story, *Peter Rabbit*, was repeatedly rejected by publishers, so she used her own money to self-publish the book.

—Madeleine L'Engle's *A Wrinkle in Time* was rejected for almost three years by publisher after publisher. Even the publisher who finally accepted it warned her that no one would buy the book. Today *A Wrinkle in Time* is in its fifty-third edition.

—Jack London received six hundred rejection letters before publishing his first story.

—Daniel Defoe self-published his books and sold them door to door.

—C. S. Lewis and J. R. R. Tolkien were writing companions. While C. S. Lewis liked *The Hobbit* series, Tolkien did not care for *The Chronicles of Narnia*, causing Lewis to stop pursuing publication.

—Rudyard Kipling was told by a newspaper editor, "I'm sorry, Mr. Kipling, but you just don't know how to use the English language."

—After numerous rejections, John Grisham self-published his first novel and sold it out of the trunk of his car.

Not only authors, but all creative artists experience rejection. Modern artists sometimes attend museum showings to watch the public laugh at their work. The first audience to hear Stravinsky's *Rite of Spring*, one of the most significant works of the past century, was so offended that they broke out in a riot. Lucille Ball dropped out of high school and was repeatedly told that she had no talent. Fred Astaire's first screen test read, "Can't act. Can't sing. Slightly bald. Can dance a little."

Walt Disney was told that no audience would sit through a full-length animated feature. Scott Joplin's father deserted his family because he was angry that Scott had decided to pursue music. Harry Lillis Crosby dropped out of school to sing with a band, much to his family's disappointment. He became Bing Crosby.

Talented, innovative people are often not accepted because their ideas are new and different, and observers do not catch the vision. After receiving numerous rejections from traditional publishing houses, many successful authors finally self-publish their first books. The following books were self-published before becoming best sellers with major publishing firms: *In Search of Excellence* by Tom Peters, *What Color Is Your Parachute?* by Richard Bolles, *The Elements of Style* by William Strunk, *The One-Minute Manager* by Ken Blanchard and Spencer Johnson, *The Christmas Box* by Richard Paul Evans, and *The Joy of Cooking* by Irma Rombauer.

Rejection is one way that artists pay their dues, become a little tougher, and grow through the experience. Creative people must believe in themselves, persevere, and be willing to fight for their dreams.

This was the challenge for our young authors: Were they going to fight? Or would they easily abandon their dreams in the face of obstacles? After our lengthy discussion, I asked the children to write about their decision and read it to the group. I knew that I had risked losing the entire writing group.

Example responses follow:

I'm not going to GIVE UP! I'm going to FIGHT! I want to pull through this. I think it would be really neat to publish a book when people keep rejecting you.

I'm going to fight!!! I really feel that this is a good book. I think if children read this story, they would like it. My partner and I will show that publisher! I'm going to FIGHT, FIGHT, FIGHT!

I'm gonna FIGHT! I really want to fight because I want to show people that children have the same talent as adults. I think the truth of publishing or not publishing my play floats somewhere between the publisher and me.

I've been thinking of fighting until I get at least five books published. But then no more writing for me because I want to get on with my life and do something else.

I'm going to fight until my book gets published. I will certainly NOT give up, because one editor out there will think my book is wonderful and will want to publish it. I will fight until the end.

I am going to fight!!! I am not going to give up. I will try over and over again until I'm an angel in heaven and even then I'm not giving up.

"Congratulations! Today you have become real authors. Never give up on your dreams or ideas," I told the writing group as we concluded our stressful session.

It Wasn't Over

As we walked out to the car, I noticed that my daughter was not speaking to me. She finally blurted out, "How could you do this to us?! I know that you are the publisher. How could you do this to my friends?!" I explained again that learning to persevere through rejection was an important part of becoming a real-life author. With a glare that could freeze time, she said those stinging words that I will never forget, "I thought I already was a real author!"

I stopped. She was right…and I was wrong. I apologized to her. She was a real author, no matter if her work was accepted for publication or not. Why should my daughter accept the world's standard of value, a world where writers are only accepted as professionals if they are financially compensated? How many potential authors had given up their dream of writing because they were denied acceptance? I thought long and hard about that question. Janelle's anger did not subside until the next day.

Rejection day was a difficult but pivotal moment in the writing group process. The children became more committed authors that day. Hopefully that lesson will last a lifetime in all their pursuits. And I became a little tougher too.

Listen carefully to first criticisms of your work. Note just what it is about your work that the critics don't like—then cultivate it. That's the only part of your work that's individual and worth keeping.

Jean Cocteau

Questions for Reflection

When have you experienced rejection?

When did you give up?

When did the rejection only make you more determined to accomplish your goal?

If there's a book you really want to read but it hasn't been written yet, then you must write it.

Toni Morrison

A writer who waits for ideal conditions under which to work will die without putting a word on paper.

E. B. White

You write or paint because you have to.
THERE IS NO CHOICE.

Maurice Sendak

Chapter 10

Completing the Publishing Process

Every book is, in an intimate sense, a circular letter to the friends of him who writes it.

Robert Louis Stevenson

With the rejection letters behind us, the writing group began to follow steps to bring their projects to completion. The young writers then submitted their proposals to a different publisher. I explained the role of agents but they were not interested in having outsiders involved, especially if the agents would share in their special rewards at the end of the process.

Acceptance letters were waiting for the children at their next meeting. I knew better than to send them a second rejection!

Negotiating the Contract

After celebrating their acceptance letters, the children's next step in the publishing process was to negotiate their contracts. The members of the writing group decided to negotiate a group contract, with the same compensation package for all. They wanted to be rewarded with a group field trip. After brainstorming many ideas, they decided to travel to Ashland, Oregon to view a Shakespearean play. The writers agreed on a deadline for submitting their completed manuscripts, to be bound into an anthology, to the publisher. They also wanted the publisher to arrange a public debut of their books: a party, complete with book signings, interviews, and the performance of one writer's play. Contracts were drawn up and signed by the children and the publisher.

The Editing Process

Motivated by the upcoming field trip, the young authors soon completed their books and submitted them for editing. Mrs. Thomas and I conferred with the children about making minor corrections and changes. The children then prepared final proofs of their books and included illustrations.

Production

Once the final pages were approved by the young writers and the publisher, the production phase of the anthology began. It was time to photocopy pages and bind them into finished products. The children designed a cover and provided short author biographies and photos for the back page.

Marketing and Sales

The job of real-life authors is often not over once the book has been produced. Publishers expect authors to help them market their books through interviews, book signings, and other publicity events.

The writing group became partners with the publisher to market their work. They wrote advertisements, complete with order forms, describing the upcoming anthology. They took orders and sold the anthology to family and friends, inviting them to a Celebration of Writing party where the anthologies would be distributed.

The young authors signed books and discussed their stories at the debut party. The children publicly interviewed one another with the aid of a mock microphone. At the end of the celebration, one writer's play was performed by the entire writing group. They had faithfully met outside of their weekly meetings to rehearse the play under the playwright's direction. From costumes to set design, the writers worked as a team to produce the play.

Farewell to the Writing Group

The writing celebration coincided with the end of the school year. Not only were the children leaving their writing group, they were also leaving their elementary school. The summer trip to Ashland was a great success and included the families of the young writers.

Upon entering the local junior high school, the writers' lives would move in different directions. Some would have English teachers who focused more on grammar exercises than inspiring the joy of creation. The transition was difficult.

Sometimes I would bring the young writers from the junior high school to their former elementary school to act as writing mentors for Mrs. Thomas' current third-grade class. They enjoyed these informal writing group reunions.

Today these former young writers are nearing completion of their college degrees and have not given up on their dreams. My daughter went on to become editor of her junior high school newspaper, copy editor of her high school yearbook, and is majoring in journalism and theater at her university. She still remembers her participation in the writing group as one of the most significant experiences in her education.

Overview

In this section, the year-long publishing process from start to finish was outlined for you to implement with your own writing group. An overview of the ten steps follows:

Step #1   Discuss the publishing process. Meet with working authors who can discuss their writing process and publishing experiences.

Step #2   Write the query letter.

Step #3   Develop the proposal, including:
- Cover letter
- Book title

- Table of contents
- Sample chapter
- Author's background and qualifications
- Market overview

Step #4   Enjoy writing the book.

Step #5   Respond to rejection or acceptance letters.

Step #6   Negotiate the contract.

Step #7   Edit the book and prepare the manuscript for publication, possibly including illustrations or photos.

Step #8   Produce the book.

Step #9   Market and sell the book. Plan events to celebrate the debut of the book.

Step #10 Celebrate the accomplishments of the writing group.

The chief glory of every people arises from its authors.
                                                    Samuel Johnson

Questions for Reflection

What part of the publication process would you find most challenging?

Which part of completing a book would you most enjoy?

Imagination is a form of knowledge.

Flannery O'Connor

You are lucky to be one of those people who wishes to build sand castles with words, who is willing to create a place where your imagination can wander.

Anne Lamott

An author's mind is a little bit like a scrap bag. If I want something, I can usually rummage around and find it. I usually think about a book for three years before I begin to write. I thought of Ramona the Pest *for fifteen years before I began to write it. I have to mull the story over and let it begin to take on a life of its own.*

Beverly Cleary

Chapter 11

More Ideas to Encourage Writing

Since writing is what generates inspiration—and not the reverse—abundant writing produces abundant inspiration.
Stephen Koch

Building on the writing group experience and publishing process as a foundation, my children enjoyed other opportunities in the coming years. They were able to continue meeting authors, tour a television news station and newspaper publishing house, create a magazine with other students, write a musical, and mentor other writers. Here are a variety of ideas to augment your exploration of the writer's world. The family writing lifestyle can be the springboard for endless creativity.

—Meet as many real-life writers as you can.

Research local author events in your newspaper. Make regular trips to meet authors and attend book signings at local bookstores. Visit newspaper publishers, radio and television news stations, and book publishers. Inquire about tours at publishing houses. Introduce your children to the real-life workings behind the author's craft. Encourage your children to correspond with authors. Children's literature authors often enjoy having contact with their fans.

—Write a play or musical.

For younger children, enacting book orchestrations is a simple way to create mini-musicals. Use a favorite book which lends itself to experimentation with sounds, song, movement, and dialogue. Read the book with your children, helping them play rhythm instruments as sound effects, sing repetitive poetry sections, dramatize the dialogue, and enact the story. An excellent example of a book which lends itself well to orchestration is Patricia Polacco's *Thundercake*. Most interesting children's books can be easily enacted. Soon your children may be creating original stories to be orchestrated.

Older children can participate in creating a play or musical. They can use familiar stories as their inspiration or write an original creation. Modernizing fairy tales is a popular vehicle for writing. The children can write scripts, make costumes, build scenery, compose music and lyrics, and audition for roles. The culmination is the performance of the work for friends and family. As a parent, don't forget to plan the cast party after the show.

—Develop a magazine or newspaper.

Your family or writing group can create a regular publication. Staff positions could include: publisher, editors, journalists, fiction writers, artists, cartoonists, photojournalists, proofreaders, graphic designers, a sales team, and recruiters for advertisements. Virginia Woolf's mother encouraged her children to publish a family newspaper.

Contributions to the publication might include:

- Advice column
- Cartoons and jokes
- Family activity ideas
- Famous quotes
- Fictional stories
- Illustrations
- Information about the month's holidays
- Interviews
- Letters to the editor
- News events

- Opinion editorials
- Opinion polls
- Photos
- Poetry
- Recipes
- Reviews of books, movies, restaurants, plays, concerts
- Travel tips and field trip information
- Word games and crossword puzzles

—Create a family newsletter.

If developing a magazine seems too ambitious, your family can create an annual newsletter, especially appropriate to send to friends and relatives during the Christmas season. Each family member can contribute their news about the year and include photos or drawings.

—Host family correspondence parties.

Some families plan correspondence parties. They sit around the kitchen table with paper, pens, decorative stickers, photos, envelopes, stamps, and other writing accessories. They write round-robin letters to relatives who live in other states. After Christmas, they write group thank-you letters. They make a family affair out of staying in touch with relatives and friends, teaching a spirit of compassion and appreciation.

I know of two families who met at a summer campground and became fast friends. The families each had four children of similar ages. They lived in opposite parts of the country so they decided to become family pen pals, with the mother writing to the mother, the father corresponding with the father, and each child writing to another child of his or her age. They corresponded throughout the year and met again at the campground the next summer. Their summer reunions have become an annual vacation event.

—Encourage your children to mentor younger writers.

Children can become "writing buddies" with other children, sharing their writing expertise with younger children who are learning. They can work on joint projects, or an older child can tutor a younger one in writing skills.

—Integrate writing into the young child's world.

For young children, it is critical to make the writing process part of their daily play. Keep paper, poster board, and pens handy as they create their make-believe worlds. My children were constantly creating complicated worlds that extended throughout our house. Often when my husband returned home from work, our furniture would be in new locations. Sometimes my children were creating restaurants, airports, train stations, markets, libraries, hair salons, business offices, and more. In their play, they included banners, signs, maps, menus, lists, letters, memos, and every imaginable form of written communication. Encourage your children to engage in creative, even sometimes outrageous, play activities.

—Develop a summer creative arts camp.

If many of the mentioned activities seem too complex to implement during the school year, you may want to dedicate a few weeks during the summer to this task. When my children were young, I hosted a summer creative arts camp as part of my piano teaching program. Sometimes the camp was one week long; other times it was two to four weeks long. I invited art, music, and dance specialists to participate. Through the years, my children and students were exposed to sculpture, watercolor painting, poetry, creative movement, historical dance forms, music theory, and music history.

You may want to enlist the help of arts experts to create summer camps with different themes. One summer you could help the children develop a musical. The next summer you could focus on different genres of literature: fiction, poetry, drama, nonfiction, etc. Another year, you could develop a summer writing group and publish books. The following summer you could produce a magazine. Perhaps you could make weekly trips to enjoy the arts by attending the ballet or theater, visiting an art museum, going to a concert, or attending authors' book signings.

Advanced writers in the teen years may even want to create their own publishing company, each specializing in editing, layout, cover design, proofing, marketing, or any of a myriad of skills required to produce a finished book.

—Develop a poetry writing program or camp.

Poetry writing is a unique specialization. Writing teachers agree that the key to learning to write poetry is immersion in reading and listening to poetry. Mrs. Thomas asked the students in her writer's workshop to memorize, read, and write poetry. When my children were young, their favorite poets were Jack Prelutsky and Shel Silverstein. Their writing group members met Jack Prelutsky at one of his poetry readings.

You may want to devote a summer camp to poetry writing. For ideas, refer to Joyce Bumgardner's book, *Helping Students Learn to Write Poetry: An Idea Book for Poets of All Ages* or *Poem-making: Ways to Begin Writing Poetry* by Myra Livingston.

Poetry writing teachers encourage students to keep poetry journals handy. They guide students in sharing their poetry with others through poetry readings or by publishing group anthologies. Bumgardner uses a tape recorder to record students reading their own poems so they can hear their creations. She also helps students create individual "poetry boxes"—decorated boxes containing special objects to inspire poetry writing. Many writing workshop leaders use unique items as writing prompts.

To become familiar with poetry terms, you can read the *Poetry Handbook* by Babette Deutsch. *The Place My Words Are Looking For* by Paul Janeczko contains a variety of poems and information about poets. This book is Bumgardner's top recommendation for writing teachers.

—**Expand your horizons.**

Encourage your children to move past self-publishing, and submit articles for publication in magazines which specialize in publishing the work of young authors. Some examples are: *Stone Soup, Word Dance, Boodle, Creative Kids, Kids' World, or Merlyn's Pen.* Look in the resource list for more information. Refer to the latest edition of *The Market Guide for Young Writers* by Kathy Henderson for numerous ideas and contacts, including writing contests.

In addition to reading good literature as models, encourage your children to read books about writing, such as *The Young Person's Guide to Becoming a Writer* by Janet Grant, *Draw and Write Your Own Picture Book* by Emily Hearn and Mark Thurman, or *Writing Your Own Plays: Creating, Adapting, Improvising* by Carol Korty.

Like singing, dancing, and play, writing may be one of those activities that all children enjoy—and enjoy learning to do better—until, all too often, they become discouraged or uninterested because something happens to inhibit their free and natural expression.

Frank Smith

No artist grows up: If he sheds the perceptions of childhood, he ceases being an artist.

Ned Rorem

Questions for Reflection

Which ideas do you want to add to your writing program? For young children? For older children? Brainstorm ideas to design the ideal summer writing arts camp.

My bursting heart must find vent at my pen.
My pen is always freer than my tongue.
My letters to you are first thoughts without correction.

Abigail Adams

Never try to think your way out of a problem, unaided by the
written word. Write your way out—in the notebook.

Stephen Koch

All writing is ultimately a question of solving a problem.

William Zinsser

Section IV

Writing
Through Life

Chapter 12

Writing as a Life Tool

Write down all the stuff you swore you'd never tell another soul.
Anne Lamott

Writing is one of the most powerful tools we can pass on to our children to navigate life's challenges. Through journaling, brainstorming, contract and letter writing, and other formats, we offer them concrete ways to strengthen relationships and handle conflicts. Writing in the home goes far beyond the obligatory thank-you note or Dear Diary experience.

Children are never too young to start writing or engage in storytelling. The writing process includes talking, imagining, doodling, and drawing pictures to communicate, and begins years before children are ready to make letters. Older siblings serve as examples for younger siblings. Children who are not introduced to the writing process before starting school have missed years of opportunities.

Journaling

First and foremost, keeping a journal is an act of honoring solitude...something very different from isolation.

Solitude is a state of being that fosters contemplation about what is at the bottom of our minds and in our hearts.
Sheila Bender
Keeping a Journal You Love

The starting point of all writing adventures and life processing begins with a personal journal or notebook. Before we can communicate with others, we must communicate and dialogue with ourselves. Compare this experience to that of a musician who must practice for hours alone before he is prepared to play in a chamber ensemble or orchestra.

A journal has been called a silent partner, a faithful companion, a safe conversation with oneself. Writers jot down ideas, often simply fragments, in notebooks. Judy Reeves says that a sketchbook is to an artist what a journal is to a writer. Stephen Koch encourages writers to "jot it all down" and describes a writer's notebook as a seedbed:

Once you've learned to recognize the seeds, you'll probably have more than you can use. With a little tending—sketching, adding, changing, seeing what moves you—some will sprout. Some will grow. Some will even make it to harvest.

The Modern Library Writer's Workshop

A four-year-old child's notebook, filled with pictures, will be different from the grief journal of a widow who has recently lost her husband to cancer or the professional writer who is collecting ideas for stories, but each is an outpouring of emotions and personal experience. We write about how we view life in a safe place without judgment, and that very process helps us adapt to new challenges.

Books about the journaling process can help you if journaling is a new experience. Virginia Hearn's *Just as I Am: Journal-Keeping for Spiritual Growth* and Sheila Bender's *Keeping a Journal You Love* are excellent guides. Somerset Maugham's *A Writer's Notebook* also offers valuable insights.

The word *journal* derives from the same root word as *journey*. Most journal methods guide writers through 1) life review and journaling about past experiences for understanding and healing; 2) journaling to examine current challenges; and 3) brainstorming about future possibilities. Ira Progoff, in *At a Journal Workshop*, describes this experience as time stretching backward and forward. We are chronicling our life's journey.

The focus of this book is on the family writing experience. While personal journals are the foundation, family communication journaling can take many different forms:

Interactive Family Journaling—Family members write letters back and forth to each other in a journal. Sometimes the entries are simply fun, and can further bond a parent and a child, or two siblings. At other times, the journal provides a safe place to deal with topics too sensitive to discuss openly. When my friend miscarried a baby, her children were grief-stricken. She was able to write individual letters to them through their interactive journals, and they were able to express their grief through writing.

Conflict Journaling—When facing a major decision or handling a disagreement, each family member can separately journal their feelings and viewpoints. This private time usually diffuses any initial "heat of the moment" anger. At a family meeting, each member can read their journal entry. The most important ground rule is that no one can interrupt while another person is reading. This is a common technique used in marriage counseling and couple workshops. You cannot listen to someone when you are interrupting them to argue or thinking about what you will say next. Journaling helps family members process their own feelings and offers a way to safely share those thoughts. It is amazing how many conflicts are resolved when people take the time to listen respectfully and understand another's point of view.

When our children were young, we would have a "writing time-out" when a serious conflict arose. One day Janelle disagreed with her dad. She wrote a set of questions for him to sit down and answer. Since my husband hates to write, he returned them with Yes/No answers. She sent him back to work, rewriting her concerns as open-ended questions. The resolution of the disagreement soon followed.

Celebration Journaling—Families often keep a travel/vacation journal to record special memories of a trip. This is usually a round-robin journal in which each family member can contribute as desired. The youngest members can draw pictures. Photos can be added later. Twenty-five years of vacation memories can be read through in a single volume. Some families keep journals in which they yearly record special events, such as birthdays, anniversaries, and holidays. When a child asks, "What did I do on my fifth birthday?" or "Where did we spend Christmas two years ago?", it's fun to consult the journal.

Large extended families who live around the country sometimes circulate a journal throughout the year. They read the preceding entries, write their own contribution, and send it on to another household. This keeps everyone connected and informed, especially aging relatives who do not have access to e-mail nor can afford expensive long distance phone bills.

Brainstorm Journaling—Every writer needs a journal for jotting down random ideas and brainstorming. Mindmapping is the most effective brainstorming method I have experienced. More important than cultivating ideas for writing projects, mindmapping is a helpful tool in problem solving and decision making. We can pour out on paper a myriad of ideas and options for tackling any issue.

In this brain-compatible method, we begin with a central focus (the center circle in the paper) and brainstorm all the possible approaches and solutions (the lines emanating from the center). For more information, you can read *Mindmapping* by J. Wycoff or *Mapping Inner Space: Learning and Teaching Mindmapping* by N. Margulies.

Imagine that your family is faced with deciding to move, due to your husband's promotion. Each family member can brainstorm their feelings and pros/cons in their journals and then come together to share their perspectives.

Perhaps your family is trying to decide where to travel this summer. Some families like to brainstorm together on a giant sheet of butcher paper with colored markers. Each member can mindmap his or her ideal vacation ideas. It's fun to consider the craziest suggestions and watch common threads emerge. Unique, memorable vacations have been planned through mindmapping that could never have been planned by a single individual. Once you are comfortable with family brainstorming sessions, you will regularly engage in this creative process.

Lifetime/Keepsake Journaling—Parents often write letters to their children to be read as adults. For example, I have kept separate journals for each of our children since their birth, in which I write letters to them on their birthdays. I write about their birthday celebrations and any special events or accomplishments during the past year. My husband, his parents, and my parents have contributed letters. Most importantly, we communicate our love for them. I know that those pages will speak to them when we are no longer here to speak in person.

Biblical Journaling—Journal writing can be an extension of our Bible study, pondering God's Word in depth. My personal approach is to read a specific Scripture passage and "write back" to God in my journal, incorporating what I have learned from Him. We can view this interactive Bible study as dialoguing with God.

Goal-setting Journaling—"Your own words are the bricks and mortar of the dreams you want to realize," stated Sonia Choquette. It is often said that the difference between goals and dreams is the steps in between. We can brainstorm short-term and long-term goals in our journals, listing concrete steps to make those dreams a reality. These may be private dreams or joint family plans.

A Harvard research study found one main difference between graduates who achieved their goals and those who did not—the young people who realized their dreams wrote them down. Seeing plans in print makes them tangible and attainable.

This could be dangerous, venturing into the private world of a writer and exposing a vein. But isn't that what journals are all about?

David Masumoto

Letter Writing

In our current culture…writing is not forbidden, it is discouraged. Hallmark does it for us.

Julia Cameron

Letters can be the fabric of intimacy between family and friends. Beatrix Potter's *Peter Rabbit* began as a story in a get-well letter to a young boy. Many authors learned how to write through writing letters. Many books have begun as letters, to someone real or imagined. Letter writing is a common device writers use when they are blocked. Writing to a specific person or audience helps our words to flow.

Letter writing can also be a consistent ministry. A friend who is recovering from cancer recently shared with me that she had saved every card and letter I sent her during our 15 years of friendship. She reads them when she needs encouragement. C. S. Lewis was well known for his ministry through the pen. In addition to book projects, he made time to correspond with numerous people. *Letters To An American Lady* is one collection of his letters, saved by the correspondent. In the preface, Clyde Kilby writes:

Yet this man meticulously endeavors to answer, sometimes with an arm so rheumatic that he can hardly push the pen, the vast correspondence falling into his hands from around the world. Why?

The main cause was that Lewis believed [that] *taking time out to advise or encourage another Christian was both a humbling of one's talents before the Lord and also as much the work of the Holy Spirit as producing a book.*

We can encourage our children to become faithful letter writers, on paper or through e-mail, which will prove invaluable in their future friendships. As children make friends on vacations or experience friends moving away, they can keep adding names to their pen pal list. Writing to relatives can be another regular occurrence.

As I was moving to a different part of the state, one of my closest friends said, "We won't stay in touch. People never do." Surprised, I said, "Of course, we will." After the move, I would write to her and sometimes leave phone messages, but I never heard from her. One day I realized that she had tried to explain to me that she didn't invest in long-distance relationships. Staying in touch with people despite distance and time is a learned habit that we can pass on to our children.

More important than encouraging our children to write letters to others are the letters we write to them. Obvious opportunities are notes put in lunches or left on their beds, or notes of congratulations for special milestones.

Anger and Apology Letters

When my eldest daughter was young, she would sometimes become quite angry with me. I decided to enforce this rule: "You may not yell at me or speak disrespectfully, but you may write anything to me." Fuming, she would go to her bedroom and pour out her anger on paper. After she had calmed down and I had read her letter, we would discuss her "issue of the moment." I have a collection of wonderful letters that I plan to give to her when she becomes a mother. To this day, when my children have a conflict with someone, they write a letter. Sometimes they send the letter; sometimes they don't. But writing gives them time to organize their thoughts and diffuse their anger before speaking to someone in person. Over time I have observed that my children (now young adults) have clean, committed relationships and know how to work through problems with people.

Apology letters have been a requirement in our house, not only to family members but to those outside our home. During her elementary school years, my daughter was involved in some late-night pranks at a sleepover which caused some damage. The next morning she was writing a letter of apology to the parents. One day my preschool son was rude to the greeter at church and he came home to write a letter of apology. Through his tears, he cried, "But why doesn't Dad have to write letters to people at church when he offends them?!"

Thank-You Letters

The dreaded thank-you note has probably done more harm to letter writing than good. No one likes to write thank-you notes, especially children, because this is a dutiful chore, not a pleasure. I grew up in a household where I wasn't allowed to play with a new toy that I had received as a gift until I wrote a letter thanking the giver. This may sound excessive in today's culture, but the message was that appreciation came first, not as an afterthought.

Letters of appreciation (not obligatory Hallmark© thank-you notes) should ideally be an outgrowth of a writing lifestyle. Mary Pipher calls these letters "essays of appreciation." I realized some years ago that perhaps my children did not understand writing letters of gratitude, because they rarely received them. They had no model. I began writing appreciation letters to them for kind acts or gifts they had given to me.

More important than thanking people for gifts is communicating to caring people the difference they have made in your life through the years. Writing tribute letters is a powerful way to show someone that you value his or her role in your life.

My children always made fun of me because I regularly sent thank-you notes and gifts to their teachers. I believe that we can never thank our children's dedicated teachers or mentors enough. Then one of my teenage daughters began receiving gifts and notes from the family of her oboe student, showing appreciation for her time and help. Finally she understood the importance of taking time to appreciate others. She had never been on the other side of that equation. Modeling is our most powerful teacher.

Communicating through heartfelt letters can be a treasured part of any relationship. Parents enjoy sending care packages with cards and gifts ("hugs through the mail") to young adult children who live away at college or serve in the military. One of my friends e-mails each of her collegiate daughters every morning with words of encouragement and love, a relevant Scripture verse, song lyrics, or a short poem. She rises early so that her messages will greet her daughters as they start their day. The power of the written word is certainly not limited to pen and paper. E-mail is the dominant written communication of our culture.

My mother was a great example to me about the beauty and power of writing as a palpable sign of love. She had seven children and, when we were off at school, she wrote to us... my mother may have said these things over the phone to me, but what stuck was that she put it on the page. She cared enough to write it.
Julia Cameron
The Right to Write

A Potpourri of Ideas for Journaling and Letter Writing

While interviewing contributors for book projects, I have been amazed to discover how many ways there are that people reach out to help friends and family through the written word. Here are some of my favorite ideas from those interviews. Enjoy the variety:

—One young newlywed couple asked every guest at their wedding reception to write a letter to them encouraging their marriage journey. Each letter was intended to be read on a different anniversary, marked by a date on the envelope.

—One couple annually takes their adult children, including wives and grandchildren, on a special trip. Upon returning, one of their daughters-in-law collects letters and photos from each family member, assembling them into a thank-you journal filled with memories to present to Grandma and Grandpa.

—One husband writes a letter of appreciation to his wife on each anniversary, thanking her for all the ways she cares for him throughout the year.

—Another husband celebrates the date of their wedding anniversary every month by leaving love notes, poems, and surprise gifts for his wife somewhere in their home.

—One daughter knew that her mom did not want to celebrate her 50th birthday with a lavish party, so she collected letters honoring her mom from close friends and family to create a 50th Landmark Birthday Journal, which far exceeded the sentiments that could have been shared at a crowded event.

—One wife sends letters to her husband's office to encourage him during a stressful day. Sometimes she includes funny cartoons. The message is always, "Thank you for working hard to take care of us."

—Another wife hides love letters and gifts in her husband's suitcase that he finds during exhausting business trips or in her children's duffle bags when they are away at summer camp.

—Before leaving for college, one daughter recorded in a journal all the significant values and traits that her parents had passed on to her. She thanked them for equipping her well for life.

—One traveling dad learned that his young children would forget important things they wanted to share with him when he phoned them in the evening or returned from a trip. To solve the dilemma, he gave his children individual journals in which they could draw or write down their thoughts. They called it the "Daddy book." Upon returning from his business trip, Dad and his children would read it together.

—One traveling mom would leave love notes and chocolate kisses hidden throughout the house for her children and husband to find during her business trips.

—One smart mother-in-law wrote a long letter to her future daughter-in-law before the wedding, encouraging her with, "You don't have to call me Mom unless you want to. You don't have to clean your house when I come over because then I will feel the need to clean my house when you visit. You don't have to spend every holiday with our family. You can create your own traditions." She warmly welcomed the new bride into their family.

—At a church retreat, the attendees were encouraged to write letters to people who had influenced their life. One young woman chose to write to her aunt who had taught her to play the piano, brought her keepsakes throughout the years, and taken her on annual trips. Those words meant so much to her aunt. The young woman learned that many people bless our lives and we need to be deliberate in telling them.

—One woman publishes a bimonthly newsletter of family news and sends it to extended family members all over the country. She keeps everyone informed of birthday celebrations, anniversaries, weddings, graduations, and more. In December she assembles a "Year in Review," complete with photos.

—One large extended family rotates a round-robin letter around the country. After one family writes their latest news, they send it on to the next family and the stories accumulate.

—One young boy was struggling with learning to read and write so his aunt became his pen pal, corresponding with him weekly and motivating him to learn.

—One woman kept a journal during her pregnancy and first year of motherhood, which she gave to her adult daughter when she was expecting her first child.

—One grandmother circulates a journal for everyone to write in at the annual family reunion. She photocopies the pages and gives each family the collection at Christmas. This tradition began five generations ago (except for the photocopies, of course). The original journal contains letters from great-great-grandmothers.

—One expectant young mother was given a "Mother-Daughter" shower as she anticipated the birth of her baby daughter. Each woman shared her best advice about the mother-daughter relationship in a journal that was rotated throughout the group.

—One mother gives jars filled with questions about their lives to older relatives. Younger children interview them as the relatives pull questions out of the jar. The children record these interviews in a journal, preserving a rich heritage.

—One woman who struggles with reaching goals writes herself a letter at the beginning of each year, encouraging herself and setting goals. She opens the letter at the end of year to evaluate her progress. Just knowing that she has to face that letter helps her keep on track.

—At a wedding shower, each guest wrote her best advice about marriage in a journal and this book of wisdom was presented to the bride-to-be.

Journal keeping and letter writing offer countless opportunities to strengthen family relationships. Don't miss this important point. The goal of writing is to build up, not tear down, relationships. Have you ever received a letter written in anger? Was it constructive? Probably not. Letters written in anger are usually only destructive. You may write them for your own coping process but do not send them. Express anger in person where the other party has a chance to discuss it immediately and resolve the problem. The pen can be poison if used inappropriately, and the words cannot be taken back.

Contracts

While journaling and letter writing can resolve conflicts, creating contracts is a proactive way to avoid future conflicts. Contracts clearly communicate parents' expectations in black-and-white print. When a child signs a contract, he or she agrees to the terms. The best results come when parents and children can negotiate the contract together. Contracts are effective for any age and any topic. The more specific the terms are, the better, avoiding confusion later. Families have used contracts for temper tantrum behavior, new driver guidelines, curfew decisions, purity commitment, abstinence from alcohol and drugs, and more. Arguments will certainly erupt in those tumultuous teen years, but referring to the original contract helps both parties.

Examples follow:

My young son's contracts were simple:

> If I yell at Mommy or throw things at her, I will be grounded and not receive any special treats for a week.
>
> Signed_____

A new driver's contract may include:

> I will drive safely and courteously, always observing the speed limit.
>
> I will abstain from alcohol and drugs.
>
> I will be home by midnight.
>
> I will transport my siblings two afternoons a week and run errands for Mom one day a week.
>
> Signed_____

Birthdays are ideal times to develop contracts. With each year, children will have more privileges as well as more responsibilities. The two go hand in hand because privileges are earned by demonstrating maturity.

The purity contracts we gave our teenage daughters on significant birthdays were more elaborate. The theme was based on their understanding that they were daughters of the King.

A Royal Promise

> *I want to live a pure life without regret.*
>
> *I will not hurt my body with drugs, cigarettes, alcohol, or other harmful substances.*
>
> *I will wait until marriage to have sex. God says this act will seal my love and commitment to my future husband.*
>
> *I do not follow these rules to earn God's love because I cannot earn God's love. He already loves me no matter what, unconditionally, in Jesus Christ. God gives me these guidelines to protect me from pain. I am a daughter of the King, a royal princess, and God wants only the best for me.*
>
> *I will wear a royal purity ring to mark today's decision.*
>
>
> *Signature_____ Date_____*

In addition to signing the contract, our daughters received purity rings they had chosen, and they received a packet of letters from significant people in their lives encouraging their journey. Some affirmed them by explaining how they had never regretted making a similar decision, and described some of the obstacles they would encounter. Others wrote letters expressing deep regret that they had not followed God as young people and the painful price they paid as a result. One young woman, who gave birth to a child out of wedlock, wrote the most powerful letter.

Memoir/Autobiography Writing

Memoir is how we try to make sense of who we are, who we once were, and what values and heritage shaped us.

William Zinsser

I have met several people in their eighties who are writing their autobiographies to pass down to their descendants. They not only want to pass down their rich experiences, but also the wisdom gained on the journey. One woman is physically unable to write down her memories so a younger friend visits her weekly to transcribe the material. Sometimes memoirs are written by grandchildren who interview their grandparents, gradually collecting the stories. Dolores Curran calls this process "family resourcing," in which healthy families hand down stories.

"Memoir narrows the lens," explains William Zinsser. Memoir writing focuses on a specific time in one's life, while autobiographical writing records a life from birth to death.

One group of sisters (now in their seventies) have been writing round-robin letters to each other since they were young women. One sister had the vision to keep those letters and has bound them into a book for all their grandchildren.

A worthwhile project is to collect stories from different grandparents and great-grandparents to create the volume, "Our Family History." Each child is a unique combination of backgrounds and genetic makeup from multiple legacies. This experience can reveal the hand of God working through generations. Scripture is certainly our example of tracing God's purpose through the lineage of families.

Three excellent resources for inspiring your own memoir writing or helping relatives record their lives are *Inventing the Truth: The Art and Craft of Memoir* by William Zinsser, *How to Write Your Own Life Story* by Lois Daniel, and *How to Write the Story of Your Life* by Frank Thomas.

Stories aren't icing; they're basic ingredients in any group that claims to be family.

Dolores Curran

Questions for Reflection

How has your family used writing as a life tool?

What ways would you like to use writing in daily life challenges?

The process of writing is always a healing process because the function of creation is always the alleviation of pain. Imagination is compassionate.

Richard Rhodes

For our writing to be healing, we must encounter something that puzzles, confuses, troubles, or pains us.

Louise DeSalvo

It is only by putting it into words that I make it whole. This wholeness means that it has lost its power to hurt me.

Virginia Woolf

Chapter 13

Writing Through Grief and Loss

The world breaks everyone and afterward many are strong at the broken places.

Ernest Hemingway

Lest you think that this book is entirely about happy family writing traditions and bonding, we never need the writing process more in our lives than when we are grieving the loss of someone we love. Loss comes in varied forms. We lose someone we love through death, divorce, or estrangement. We lose friends and family through life changes, such as moves or a child leaving for college. We may lose loved ones, but we do not have to lose communicating our love to them. We can write through our pain, discovering that the written word will help to heal us.

C. S. Lewis wrote *A Grief Observed* to cope with losing his wife. Sheldon Vanauken wrote the powerful *A Severe Mercy* after his wife died. Roald Dahl wrote in his memoirs about losing his daughter to encephalitis. D. H. Lawrence wrote poems about his dying mother as he sat by her bedside. Anne Lamott wrote her first novel as a love letter to her dad, chronicling his battle with cancer. They worked on the project together as his death approached. Dave Pelzer wrote *A Child Called "It"* to deal with his childhood abuse. Julia Cameron began the ritual of writing three pages longhand every morning while she was living through a painful divorce. She called them "mentoring pages."

Mary Shelley lost both her son and daughter within two years. Her harsh husband and father found her grief unacceptable, a sign of weakness, and Shelley was contemplating suicide when she turned to writing to relieve her despair. Writers must express their grief, and often the writing page is the only safe place to mourn.

Writing is certainly not limited to paper. One woman made a quilt for her friend who had lost her husband. At the funeral, every guest wrote a special memory about this man on a quilt square. The widow said that she literally could wrap herself up in treasured memories on the hardest days. Other friends have used journals at memorial services to collect remembrances for grievers.

Many grievers have told me that the best gifts they received after losing loved ones were long letters from friends, sharing detailed memories of their beloved. Letters are not intrusive. They are not knocks on the door when we do not want to see anyone. Letters can be opened when we are ready and are permanent gifts that can be read repeatedly to comfort us. Compassionate letters only give and never take.

Writing is medicine. It is an appropriate antidote to injury. It is an appropriate companion for any difficult change.
Julia Cameron

Letters of Grief

Death ends a life, but it does not end a relationship.
Robert Anderson

The most common way that we can grieve is to write letters or journal entries to our lost loved ones. When we write to someone, we are talking to them on paper. *An Early Journey Home: Helping Families Grieve the Loss of a Child*, inspired by my therapy work with terminally ill patients in a children's hospital, is filled with letters written by parents to their deceased children, or journal entries about their experience.

Widows write to deceased husbands; children write to parents; friends write to lost friends. We need to say things to people that we never had a chance to say when they were alive. We write to say final goodbyes. Interactive journaling between family members helps express and release grief when the pain is too fresh to discuss.

My teenage daughter recently lost her good friend, Hayley, to cystic fibrosis. My daughter and her friends wrote and decorated posters honoring Hayley, and wrote good-bye letters to her. They created a keepsake quilt for her parents. They even wrote messages to Hayley on the rear windows of their cars, displayed for the entire town to view. Hayley's memorial service was a loving tribute. Poems written by her friends were recited, letters were read, and songs were sung. The written word is a powerful healer.

Everyone grieves in different ways. Hayley's parents did not want to be alone, and frequently invited Hayley's teenage friends into their home in the evenings. During high school, my husband's father and younger brother were killed in a lake accident. My husband and his mom, also extroverted social people, did not want to be alone. Neither would have been comforted by the introspective writing process.

We introverts tend to be more comforted by putting pen to paper in our grief, which I personally experienced when my dad died. He went to the hospital for a simple angiogram and the next day underwent major cardiac surgery. He never regained consciousness and died a few days later. I was quite close to him, and writing was critical to my healing.

First I wrote a letter honoring my dad, which my husband graciously read at my dad's memorial service because I did not have the strength to read it. Then I began writing letters daily to my dad in a journal, proceeding to weekly, and finally monthly. Since I had traveled to another part of the state to be with my dad during his emergency surgery, I left my hometown. Many of my friends had helped with countless details during my absence and I did not have the energy to personally call to thank each one and explain my dad's death. So again I wrote a letter to my friends and talked to everyone through the mail. I do not know how I would have survived this rugged time in my life without the writing process.

My dad died on a Wednesday. Every Wednesday for the first year of my grief, one close friend left garden flowers and comforting notes on my porch. Her message was: "I remember your pain. Hope in the spring to come during the winter of your soul." Kind words are truly a honeycomb for the soul.

I know of one woman with terminal cancer who wrote letters to each of her adult children and lifelong friends, expressing how special they were to her and how much she loved them, to be opened after her death. Other people facing death have communicated to loved ones through recorded tapes. We long for tangible remembrances of people we have loved and lost.

My husband treasures the last note that his deceased brother left for him on the refrigerator. It simply said, "I'm sorry I drank the last Dr. Pepper. Love, Mark." Such a simple act would never be forgotten.

One close friend also lost her father to heart disease. One moment her father was an active, vibrant man, and the next moment he was dead from a heart attack. There were no final good-byes. My friend felt comfortable speaking at his well-attended funeral, but was not as comfortable writing his eulogy. She invited me to her home and we spent the evening crying together and talking about her best memories about her dad. I went home to write the eulogy that she would read at his service. Walking through my friend's pain with her was one of the greatest privileges I have known as a writer.

We write to work through our grief. We write to comfort others as they grieve. Kind words are always welcomed. Counselors encourage clients to grieve their losses through writing. Sometimes cancer patients dialogue with their changing bodies in a journal. One unwed teenage birth-mother wrote a letter to the child she gave up for adoption, to be opened when the child was eighteen years old.

Wives write letters to divorced husbands; parents write to estranged teens; adults write to parents who neglected or abused them as children. These letters are rarely sent, yet help the writer to understand his or her pain and forgive those who caused it.

Writing is a friend whose shoulder we can cry on. Writing is a confidant who listens and lets us sort things out. Writing is a comrade, marching with us through the steep days of sorrow and despair.

Julia Cameron
The Right to Write

Writing to Forgive

The act of writing about something painful can help right a wrong that has been done to you. It can be a form of restitution.
Louise DeSalvo
Writing as a Way of Healing

Forgiveness is a unique form of grief work, which involves examining very real losses in our lives. Forgiving someone who injured us is critical to our own healing and recovery. One close friend, who lost a daughter to cancer and a husband to divorce, shared with me that the loss of her marriage was more painful, because "the corpse was still walking around."

Forgiveness is hard work. It is a choice, not a feeling. When we do not have the opportunity to forgive our offenders in person, we can still forgive them in writing. Sometimes sending the letter is healing for both parties. At other times it may not be safe to send the letter. Contacting an abusive ex-spouse could be dangerous; and sometimes the person we need to forgive is deceased.

"Forgive and forget" can be misleading, because we must fully remember in order to fully forgive, and only then can we forget. For authentic forgiveness and healing to take place, we must remember everything to be able to let go of it. True forgiveness involves closely examining the root of our pain and unlocking its hold on our lives through forgiving the one who wounded us. Many people find writing to be the most effective route to permanent forgiveness.

We can also seek forgiveness through writing. My husband was betrayed by a business associate, considered to be a close friend, many years ago. The associate, "Steve," joined a different company, which sued my husband. Soon after, Steve's wife divorced him, discovering that he had been involved in multiple affairs. Steve had led a double life that no one knew about. Years later, my husband received a letter from Steve asking for forgiveness for his wrongdoings. Steve had learned that he was dying of cancer.

When we genuinely forgive, we set a prisoner free and then discover that the prisoner we set free was us.

We are never so free as when we reach back into our past and forgive a person who caused us pain. We cannot erase the past; we can only heal the pain it has left behind.

Lewis Smedes

Legacies and Ritual Wills

We are familiar with legal wills, but wills of the heart can be more important in our lives. Written ethical wills are derived from Jewish tradition, communicating the values that we want our children to inherit. Ethical wills do not hand down material possessions and property. They offer a gift far more valuable—sharing with our children what is important to us and how we hope they will live their lives. Ethical wills can be presented to a loved one at any time in life, not only upon someone's death.

Ritual wills spell out what a dying person's wishes are for a burial service and the months to come. One woman in the final stages of cancer planned a private memorial service at the beach. She knew that her children and grandchildren loved the ocean and would need a day of retreat. She requested that her ashes be spread on the water.

This dying mother wrote out specific recipes for the meal to follow, all favorite dishes of her children. It was her final gift to them. She wrote to close friends, asking them to reach out to her children on her birthday and Mother's Day.

Writing to Heal From Loss

Writing...has been a sturdy ladder out of a deep pit.

Alice Walker

Alice Walker, who struggled with suicidal depression, said that she could write or she could kill herself. Ernest Hemingway, Virginia Woolf, and Sylvia Plath did both. Does writing prevent suicide? Of course not. Yet writing can help us heal.

Loss of a loved one to death, loss of a childhood at the hands of an abusive parent, loss of a marriage because of an unfaithful spouse…loss has been the reason that many hurting people, who never intended to become professional authors, began writing. The words they wrote to heal from their own wounds became vehicles to help others.

As a creative arts therapist, I've always known that verbalization and creative expression are keys to coping and healing. Life review, painting a life portrait, is important for each of us. Having experienced this process in different classes and workshops, I never cease to discover another revelation, described by many as being like peeling another layer off an onion. Writing helps us step back and reexamine life in totality, including the good and the bad, and connecting the past and the future. We look at our actions today, how they are influenced by our past, and how we can change them in the future.

Dr. DeSalvo wisely cautions us that the key to healing is writing about the past without poisoning the present. Dealing with traumatic memories is best done with the support and guidance of a skilled therapist.

All writers simply know that they feel better after they pour their thoughts out on paper. Patient, derived from the Latin word *patiens*, means to suffer. Perhaps the best description of a writer is a suffering healer.

Many writers come to their craft only after they have been shattered by life in some way.

Christopher Vogler

Questions for Reflection

How have you coped with loss and grief in your life?

Which method has been most effective?

Have you ever written a letter to someone with no intention of sending it?

Writing. A gift that comes to us.
A gift we give ourselves.
A gift we give to others.

Louise DeSalvo

The more I wrote, the more I became a human being.
Henry Miller

Writing is my way of celebrating life and my way of escaping despair. When I am having a grumpy day, it is usually because I haven't written.
Donald Murray

Section V

The Importance of the Family Writing Lifestyle

Chapter 14

Nurturing the Family Writing Lifestyle: Why Bother?

*Children don't merely love family rituals, with its wondrous combination of predictability and specialness; they **need** it.*

Good family rituals can be a steadying compass in today's fragmented culture.

Ritual is an anchor, a home base.

Meg Cox
The Heart of a Family

Before proceeding any further, let's stop to ask an important question, "Why bother?" In the chaos and stress of our already too busy lives, aren't these extra activities simply icing on the cake, among the frills and fluff of life? If we are going to invest this much time and energy in nurturing our families, is it worth all the effort? Definitely, yes.

You may remember a revolutionary book published in 1983, entitled *Traits of a Healthy Family* by Dolores Curran. DeFrain's and Stinett's *Secrets of Strong Families* followed in 1985. These books were groundbreaking because they explored what was right with families instead of studying what was wrong with families. These researchers proposed a healthy model in family studies vs. the traditional illness model.

Curran's research produced a list of fifteen traits common to healthy families which still apply today. Three of her ground-breaking observations were:

—The healthy family has a strong sense of family in which rituals and traditions abound.

—The healthy family communicates and listens.

—The healthy family fosters table time and conversations.

These statements may sound like plain common sense, yet families are struggling today to hold on to these basic values. What intrigues me most is that these dated revelations were considered revolutionary research twenty years ago. Any connected family inherently knows that rituals and celebrations of life are not frivolous extras. They are the foundation, our anchor in the monsoons of life. Unique traditions bind our families together today, and more importantly, in the future to come.

Through the years, psychologists and family researchers have given this anchor several labels: family identity, bonding, a sense of community, and belonging. Children label it far more succinctly. It is: "eating pizza and watching a movie every Friday night" or "when Mom puts notes in my lunch" or "on rainy Saturday nights, we make s'mores and tell stories around the fire." We know it when we see it.

We also know that teens long for belonging and identity. If they do not find it in their families of origin, they will seek it in their peer groups, whether they are healthy or unhealthy.

Tradition is family insurance against outside pressures that threaten to overwhelm our days and weaken our ties to each other.

Susan Lieberman

Resiliency

Writing regularly fosters resilience—a quality that enables people subjected to difficulties to thrive despite them...signaling that we have chosen hope rather than despair.

Louise DeSalvo

Resilient materials return to their original state after enduring compressed stress without rupturing. Researchers, building on the study of healthy family characteristics, have spent the past decade studying why certain people bounce back after enduring crisis and adversity, while others do not recover. Bonnie Benard, a pioneer in resiliency research, began focusing on the positive factors in resilient young people instead of the negative factors. The theme of resiliency work is communicating to children that what is right with them is stronger than what is wrong with them, called the "resiliency attitude."

Advocates agree that fostering resiliency in young people is a process, not a program, and developing healthy, supportive relationships is the key. Even in the most stable, loving families, young people must learn to recover from life's disappointments and crises. This process applies to all children, and should not be limited to "at-risk kids," a label which has actually done more harm than good. Resilient young people thrive in mentor-rich environments and safe, caring communities. Is this not the best definition of a healthy, connected family? Fran Stott sums it up:

Children need more than food, shelter, and clothing. They need at least one person who is crazy about them.

Frills or Foundation?

Allow me to borrow an example from the child life field. Working in a children's hospital, I learned firsthand that what are sometimes perceived as frills by outsiders are often actually foundational. Before the child life field was established, hospitalized children were separated from their families. They received medical treatment for their illnesses, but social/emotional or educational programs were unavailable. Parents could not spend the night and were limited to visiting hours. No one took the time to explain scary procedures to patients. Play therapy and crisis counseling were absent. Children were cut off from their normal lives. Though their health would slowly improve, pediatric patients were often depressed, angry, scared, and miserable.

Then a remarkable thing happened. Innovative doctors and nurses noticed that happier children recovered faster. Child life programs were introduced into children's hospitals, where patients could play, laugh, paint, draw, make music, write, continue their school work, and much more. Through these therapeutic activities, children learned to cope with their illnesses, celebrate life with other patients, and have fun. Hospital administrators who initially thought that child life programs were an unnecessary waste of money learned that they couldn't afford **not** to have such programs.

Our families deserve the same investment. Similar to pediatric patients, our children must learn to cope with life's unexpected twists and turns. We cannot prevent life's challenges, but we can help prepare our children to face them. Coping skills are learned at home. Investing in a child's emotional well-being always pays off, especially in the crises of life. My own daughter, who has experienced painful challenges through caring for friends, once told me, "As long as your home is a stable, safe place, you can handle almost anything in the outside world."

While interviewing contributors for *What to Do When You Don't Know What to Say*, my coauthor and I made an amazing discovery. We learned that many people find it easier to care for friends, acquaintances, and even complete strangers in crisis than it is to perform acts of TLC for their own family members. That discovery prompted the sequel, *What to Do When You Don't Know What to Say to Your Own Family*, studying how family members reach out to one another through the crises of life.

The sequel revealed another unexpected gem. A handful of thoughtful acts sprinkled throughout the year didn't make a dent. Healthy families nurtured members with habitual caring acts, rituals that were like "relationship glue" through the ups and downs of life. Prevention is the best medicine for most physical diseases, and the same is true for our families. The time to start developing family connection rituals is not *during* a crisis. That is too late. Relationship glue activities must already be in place. Family therapist William Doherty calls this "intentional family."

One publisher rejected this book with the following reproach, "These are great ideas but families don't have time for extras. Families today are simply trying to survive and troubleshoot." Perhaps that is our fast-paced culture's problem. These so-called extras are not a priority. This viewpoint is analogous to a company which is constantly engaged in crisis management, but never practices any visionary planning. To view traditions and family activities as icing on the cake when life is going smoothly is backwards. Families most need their bonds of tradition when life spirals out of control.

Did you know that...

—The National Center on Addiction and Substance Abuse found that young people who regularly eat dinner with their families are less likely to abuse drugs and alcohol?

—Steven Wolin, a psychiatrist and researcher, researched rituals in families with a history of alcoholism. He discovered that the more committed a family was to its traditions, the less likely the alcoholism would be passed on to the next generation?

—Recent research shows that one of the best predictors of high SAT scores and academic excellence is the time spent eating meals together as a family?

—In a survey of couples married over fifty years, the couples credited eating dinner together every night (even after their children left home) as one of the main factors contributing to their lasting marriage?

Relational Traditions

Hope is what we need so badly, and hope is based in the memory. Rituals do much to feed that hope through memory. And hope is the travel virtue—it gets us from yesterday into today and gives us the courage to face tomorrow.

Claire Bernreuter

Your greatest obstacle to creating lasting family rituals may be perceiving tradition making as time-consuming fluff. Walk into any bookstore and you will see colorful books and glossy magazines about traditions, impressive decorations, cooking, table settings, holiday crafts, and more. You need to rid yourself of erroneous preconceptions if you are going to weave meaningful traditions, especially writing rituals, into daily life.

When I became a mother, I was curious to know if the same techniques I used as a creative arts therapist with hospitalized patients would transfer to the home. Realizing that parents are professional nurturers,

I read volumes about family bonding, rituals, and traditions, but rarely found a concrete answer to the question, "What do I realistically do today?" I was searching for realistic traditions, activities that would keep my family glued together when life was far from perfect.

Worthwhile rituals are based in relationship. Relational traditions shout to our children, "You are treasured. I have time for you. You hold a special place in our family." Why we develop family activities is far more important than what we do. If you love to cook, decorate, give parties, and are energized by all the preparations, knock yourself out. Often children enjoy participating. But if such activities drain you and take time away from developing relationships with your children, **stop**. We do not want merely the display of traditions in our lives. We want to build rituals of the heart. Writing traditions are ideal relational traditions.

Here is an easy test for your current traditions:

- Does this activity tire you, or energize you?
- Does it encourage family bonding, or family conflict?
- Do your children feel special, or overlooked?
- Do your children participate because they want to, or because they have to?

If you are tired and stressed and your children feel left out, then something is wrong. I know one woman who sends her children to the daycare center or babysitter so that she can clean house, shop, decorate, set the table, and prepare holiday dinners for twenty people. Is this a relational tradition?

Relational traditions are literally not picture perfect. Throw away those glossy magazines.

Mini-Retreats

Think of your favorite traditions, most loved by your family. I would imagine that they pass this relational profile test:

- Relational traditions are mini-retreats in the chaos of life. They provide a family oasis. These activities connect family members, not separate them.

• Relational traditions are not imposed or forced but are natural out-growths of healthy family time.

• Relational traditions build many little daily bridges, not walls.

• Relational traditions are love-bound, not duty-bound.

• Relational traditions reduce the stress of life, not increase it.

• Relational traditions are "keepers" and have stood the test of time.

• Relational traditions are fluid, changing with the needs of family members and growing children.

• Relational traditions are comforting, nurturing, therapeutic "glue."

Do you want the display of traditions in your home (these look very good to outside observers), or traditions which develop sustaining relationships? These are two very different goals.

We want to build bridges, treasuring the past and reaching for the future.

One Final Misconception

The entire purpose of building family rituals, especially writing rituals, is to develop relationships. Do not misunderstand this goal. It is not to create ideal families or perfect, successful children. Parents are not that powerful. Traditions are not an insurance policy or a guaranteed formula for the perfect family life.

I know children who grew up in Christian families with lavish traditions who have struggled in life. I know children who grew up in Christian families with few traditions and less nurturing who are capable, resilient adults. There are no formulas.

Life is unavoidably painful...loved ones die...couples divorce...friends betray one another...car accidents occur...teenage girls become pregnant...teens become involved with drugs or alcohol...others contemplate suicide, and some succeed. Parents try their very best to create a safe haven at home for their children, but there are no guarantees. We build a family identity of relational traditions to ground them when life's challenges come. Our hope is that all the little bridges will hold up over turbulent waters.

No formula for healthy families exists, but hopefully we can offer memories filled with security and love that will stand the test of time and help our families stay connected.

Questions for Reflection

Why is it important to plan time to connect as a family?

Think about some of your favorite family rituals. Are they relational traditions?

We walk by faith, not by sight. Life without imagination is life without faith.

Alvin Dueck and Gabrielle Taylor

When you speak, your words echo only across the room or down the hall. But when you write, your words echo down the ages.

Bud Gardner

Words are clothes that thoughts wear.

Samuel Butler

Chapter 15

What Does God Say?

A Biblical View of Writing and Family Traditions

As it is written…
Written for generations to come…
And the Word became flesh and dwelled among us…

Researchers and educators may convince you that the role of writing and family bonding is critical to nurturing families, but what does God say? In *Music Education in the Christian Home*, we learned that over two hundred Scripture references direct us to make music to God. Learning to make music is a command from God, not an extracurricular hobby. Over fourteen hundred references to writing (or words) appear in Scripture. Through narrative, poetry, and letters, the Bible is a comprehensive guidebook to the writing process. Why are words so powerful?

The written word is life-changing and powerful because it is **permanent**. Legal documents are drawn up in written form. Wills are considered binding unless a second document is found. Graduation certificates and degrees are suitable for framing. Marriage ceremonies require licenses. We laugh when young people say that they don't need a piece of paper to love each other for a lifetime. Only when they are willing to sign that piece of paper do they understand the permanency of love and commitment.

Whenever we negotiate a contract, we hear the words, "Put it in writing." Our written signature is our word. Talk is cheap; the written word is permanent and lasting.

"Your name is written in the Book of Life" is the most comforting statement a person can read. Writers especially understand how much our unchanging God loves us when we read those words.

God's Word is His oath. Read Deuteronomy 31:19–22. God instructs Moses:

"Now write down this song which you must use; teach it to the sons of Israel, put it into their mouths that it may be a witness on my behalf against the sons of Israel...Yes, even today, before I have brought him to the land I promised on oath, I know what plans he has in mind." So on that same day, Moses wrote out this song and taught it to the sons of Israel. (Deuteronomy 31:19)

I have personally viewed Scripture as God's love letters to His children, to **me**. More amazing is that God would describe Himself as the Word, in language terms.

In the beginning was the Word, and the Word was with God, and the Word was God.

John 1:1

Broken Tablets

Moses made his way back down the mountain with the two tablets of the Testimony in his hands, tablets inscribed on both sides, inscribed on the front and on the back. These tablets were the work of God, and the writing on them was God's writing engraved on the tablets.

Exodus 32:15–16

God is a writer. When God delivered a message, he did it in writing. He provided us with a permanent record of the history of His people. He continues today to reach people through His written word. Read the above verse and then notice what occurs in the next verse. When Moses returned to camp, he found God's people worshipping idols. ...*Moses' anger blazed. He threw down the tablets he was holding and broke them at the foot of the mountain* (Exodus 32:19–20). Moses would not allow God's Word to be mocked.

But God is a persistent writer. He said to Moses: *Cut two tablets of stone like the first ones and come up to Me on the mountain, and I will inscribe on them the words that were on the first tablets, which you broke.* God never gives up on us.

Have you ever lost a finished document on your computer and had to start all over again from scratch? God knows your frustration.

Not taking God's Word seriously is dangerous business. Trying to eliminate God's Word is disastrous. Read Jeremiah 36:11–32. Jeremiah and Baruch feared for their lives. Jeremiah dictated God's Word to Baruch, who wrote it down in ink on the scroll that was read to the people. The king sent for the scroll and threw it into the fire, piece by piece, as it was read. God hid Baruch and Jeremiah, telling them: *Take another scroll and write down all the words that were written on the first scroll burned by Jehoiakim king of Judah* (v. 28). God promised to punish the king: *I will punish him, his heirs and his servants for their misdeeds; on them, on the citizens of Jerusalem and on the men of Judah I will bring down all the disasters with which I have threatened them, though they have not listened* (v. 31).

Take off your theological glasses for a moment and view God in a radical new way. Think about God as a writer—the ultimate writer. Be deeply moved that, of all the ways God could have chosen to communicate with us through the ages, He chose the written word, which is final evidence of a permanent relationship. God only chooses the best for us. Let it sink in that Jesus Christ is the Word incarnate, the Word who became flesh and dwelt among us.

Written on our Hearts

God not only writes on stone tablets and in the Book of Life, God writes on our hearts:

Deep within them I will plant my Law, writing it on their hearts. Then I will be their God and they shall be my people.
Jeremiah 31:33b

You yourselves are our letter, written on our hearts, known and read by everybody. You show that you are a letter from Christ,

*the result of our ministry, written not with ink, but with the Spirit
of the living God, not on tablets of stone, but on tablets of human
hearts.*

2 Corinthians 3:2–3

We are living letters from Christ, written to a hurting world. What
God writes on our hearts is intended to be shared with others.

*You shall love Yahweh your God with all your heart, with all your
soul, with all your strength. Let these words I urge on you today
be written on your heart. You shall repeat them to your children
and say them over to them whether at rest in your house or walking abroad, at your lying down or at your rising; you shall fasten
them on your hand as a sign and on your forehead as a circlet;
you shall write them on the doorposts of your house and on your
gates.*

Deuteronomy 6:5–9

As parents, the most important people to share this writing on our
hearts with is our children. Sunday morning faith simply won't cut it. We
need to share these words with them in our home and away from home,
when we get up in the morning and when we go to sleep at night (i.e., all
day). God knows how easily distracted we become, so He encourages us
to use rituals and visible reminders of our faith in our homes and on our
person.

*"Keep the pieces of wood you have written on in your hand where
they can see..."*

Ezekiel 37:20

A mentor relationship and setting an example are never more important than when we model consistent Scripture reading for our children. I
know of one woman who kept her Bible open on her kitchen counter to
make Scripture relevant to real life. She and her family referred to passages throughout each day as situations arose.

The Power of Words

Nathaniel Hawthorne said, "Words—so innocent and powerless as
they are, as standing in a dictionary, how potent for good and evil they

become in the hands of one who knows how to combine them." Words can do great good and great harm. One of the greatest lies you learned as a child was: "Sticks and stones may break my bones, but words can never hurt me."

God's Word teaches us that kind words can be as a honeycomb to the soul (Proverbs 16:24). Words comfort and heal us. Yet words can also tear us to shreds (Hosea 6:5).

As someone who loves to write and receive letters, I am impressed that half of the New Testament, the foundation of our faith, consists of letters, correspondence between flesh-and-blood people who struggled like you and I have.

God's written word has multiple purposes: to encourage, teach, correct, rebuke, prepare us, and give us hope. Finally, God's Word is intended to be fulfilled. God's written word is truthful. Have you ever read an account written by a journalist who did not have all the facts correct? God's Word is infallible.

For everything that was written in the past was written to teach us, so that through endurance and the encouragement of the Scriptures we might have hope.

Romans 15:4

Therefore encourage each other with these words.

1 Thessalonians 4:18

Preach the Word; be prepared in season and out of season; correct, rebuke and encourage—with great patience and careful instruction.

2 Timothy 4:2

(Jesus said,) "What is written about me is reaching its fulfillment."

Luke 22:37

Writers often define writing as "talking on paper." The spoken word is as powerful as the written word. Again, we are Christ's letter to the world:

Be wise in the way you act toward outsiders; make the most of every opportunity. Let your conversation be always full of grace, seasoned with salt, so that you may know how to answer everyone.

Colossians 4:5–6

Do not let any unwholesome talk come out of your mouths, but only what is helpful for building others up according to their needs, that it may benefit those who listen.

Ephesians 4:29

But now you must rid yourselves of all such things as these: anger, rage, malice, slander, filthy language from your lips.

Colossians 3:8

...no man can tame the tongue. It is a restless evil, full of deadly poison...Out of the same mouth come praise and cursing. My brothers, this should not be.

James 3:8, 10

The way we use language, for good or evil, is a window into our relationship with God.

Frustrated Writers

One last thing, my son, be warned that writing books involves endless hard work, and that much study wearies the body.

Ecclesiastes 12:12

Lest you imagine biblical writers as angelic scribes who never struggled with the writing process, realize that they were real people with real frustrations.

In both Second and Third John, the letter ends with the same message:

I have much to write you, but I do not want to do so with pen and ink. I hope to see you soon, and we will talk face to face.

Translation: "Forget the writing. I want to talk to you in person."

Paul's intensity and temper pervades his letters. In Galatians 6:11, he explodes: *See what large letters I use as I write to you with my own hand!*

Translation: "I am not fooling around now." There was steam coming off the page.

Paul knew that his letters were not always welcomed. Paul was not immune to criticism. In 2 Corinthians 10:9–11, he writes:

I do not want to seem to be trying to frighten you with my letters. For some say, "His letters are weighty and forceful, but in person he is unimpressive and his speaking amounts to nothing." Such people should realize that what we are in our letters when we are absent, we will be in our actions when we are present.

I completely identify with Paul, someone who was criticized as being better on paper than in person.

Writing was at the core of the biblical Christian community. In *Life Together*, Dietrich Bonhoeffer explains:

The measure with which God bestows the gift of visible community is varied. The Christian in exile is comforted by a brief visit of a Christian brother, a prayer together and a brother's blessing; indeed, he is strengthened by a letter written by the hand of a Christian. The greetings in the letters written with Paul's own hand were doubtless tokens of such community.

Writing Devotions

To explore the role of writing in Scripture further, you may want to use the above verses in addition to the following verses as family devotions or writing prompts for journaling. Both will, hopefully, lead to some interesting discussions. View the writing process through the "eyes" of Scripture. Old Testament verses quoted are from the *Old Jerusalem Bible,* while New Testament verses are from the *New International Version.* Read the entire chapter first to understand the context of each passage. I have emphasized words that are relevant to writing.

*When you were dead in your sins and in the uncircumcision of your sinful nature, God made you alive with Christ. He forgave us all our sins, having canceled the **written** code, with its regulations, that was against us and that stood opposed to us; he took it away, nailing it to the cross.* Colossians 2:13b–14

*Let the **word** of Christ dwell in you richly as you teach and counsel one another with all wisdom, and as you sing psalms, hymns and spiritual songs with gratitude in your hearts to God.* Colossians 3:16

*Then Yahweh answered and said, "**Write** the vision down, **inscribe** it on tablets to be easily read, since this vision is for its own time only: eager for its own fulfillment, it does not deceive; if it comes slowly, wait, for come it will, without fail.* Habakkuk 2:2, 3

*Ah, would that these words of mine were **written** down, **inscribed** on some monument with iron chisel and engraving tool, cut into the rock for ever.* Job 19: 23, 24

*But they deliberately forget that long ago by God's **word** the heavens existed and the earth was formed out of water and with water.* 2 Peter 3:5

*Listen, my son, take my **words** to heart, and the years of your life shall be multiplied.* Proverbs 4:10

*You had scrutinized my every action, all were **recorded in your book**, my days listed and determined, even before the first of them occurred.* Psalms 139:16

*Blessed is the one who reads the **words** of this prophecy, and blessed are those who hear it and take to heart what is **written** in it, because the time is near.* Revelation 1:3

*Nothing impure will ever enter it, nor will anyone who does what is shameful or deceitful, but only those whose names are **written** in the Lamb's **book** of life.*

Revelation 21:27

*Moses **recorded** their starting points in **writing** whenever they broke camp on Yahweh's orders.*

Numbers 33:2a

*Kind **words** are a honeycomb, sweet to the taste, wholesome to the body.*

Proverbs 16:24

*"O king, ratify the edict at once by **signing** this document, making it unalterable, as befits the law of the Medes and the Persians, which cannot be revoked."*

Daniel 6:8

*At that time Michael will stand up, the great prince who mounts guard over your people. There is going to be a time of great distress, unparalleled since nations first came into existence. When that time comes, your own people will be spared, all those whose names are found **written** in the **Book**. Of those who lie sleeping in the dust of the earth many will awake, some to everlasting life, some to shame and everlasting disgrace. The learned will shine as brightly as the vault of heaven, and those who have instructed many in virtue, as bright as stars for all eternity.*

Daniel 12:13

*The **word** addressed to Jeremiah by Yahweh: Yahweh, the God of Israel says this: **Write** all the **words** I have spoken to you in a **book**. For see, the days are coming—it is Yahweh who speaks— when I will restore the fortunes of my people Israel (and Judah), Yahweh says, and bring them back to possess the land I gave to their ancestors.*

Jeremiah 30:1–3

*How dare you say: We are wise, and we possess the Law of Yahweh? But look how it has been falsified by the **lying pen** of the* *scribes! The wise shall be shamed, caught out, confounded. Look how they have rejected the **word** of Yahweh! So what use is their wisdom to them?*

Jeremiah 8:8, 9

*Jeremiah then gave Baruch this order: "As I am prevented from entering the Temple of Yahweh, you yourself must go and, from the **scroll** you **wrote** at my dictation, read all the **words** of Yahweh to the men of Judah who come in from the towns. Perhaps they will offer their prayers to Yahweh and each one turn from his evil way, for great is the anger and wrath with which Yahweh has threatened this people."*

Jeremiah 36:5b–7

*Samuel explained the royal constitution to the people and **inscribed** it in a **book**, which he placed before Yahweh.*

1 Samuel 10:25

*The Lord Yahweh says this: There will be no further delay in the fulfilling of any of my **words**. What I say is said and will come true—it is the Lord Yahweh who speaks.*

Ezekiel 12:28b

Behold, I have inscribed you on the palms of my hands...

Isaiah 49:16 NASB

Someone who wants to write but doesn't love to read is like someone who talks and never listens.

Lisa Glatt

The library was my education. I was taught by the literary imaginations of others. It's impossible to learn any other way. The only school for a writer is the library—reading, reading.

Nadine Gordimer

A book ought to be an ice pick to break up the frozen sea within us.

Franz Kafka

Chapter 16

A Wake-up Call for Parents About Literacy

Henry David Thoreau observed that people live lives of "quiet desperation," but today a better description is aimless distraction.
Rick Warren

In previous chapters, we have looked at what family researchers say and what God says about grounding families. Now we will observe what our culture says.

For a terrifying wake-up call for parents, read Sven Birkerts' *The Gutenberg Elegies: The Fate of Reading in an Electronic Age* or Mary Pipher's *The Shelter of Each Other*. These authors alert us that we are in the midst of a crisis. We live in an electronic culture where screen attachment is considered normal behavior. Sociologists voice concerns that the more electronically connected we become as a society, the more isolation we experience as individuals.

Our children's companions are televisions, computers, Nintendo sets, CD-ROMs, and other technological devices. Cell phones invade alone time, such as driving or walking, that was once a retreat for daydreaming and uninterrupted thinking. Family vans are now equipped with televisions. Families may no longer fight in the car, but they don't talk either. One phone company recently began broadcasting channels on cell phones so that customers can watch television no matter where they are. High-powered graphics make sports video games more attractive than actually playing outside. Sometimes young people today have more consistent relationships with machines than with people, or through machines with people.

Young people are not alone in their electronic relationships. I met my husband the old-fashioned way (in person, in college) but many of my mid-life divorced friends (male and female) are finding their second mates through electronic dating services and Internet chat rooms. As one friend explained, "You can find out if someone is potentially compatible without investing all that time to find out he is not." Beyond Internet chatting, many young singles are finding romance in fantasy multiplayer on-line games. One advertisement explains:

If you are looking for Prince Charming...this role-playing world is fast attracting single young people, the ones who are more comfortable acting out their fantasies or engaging in social situations behind a computer monitor than face to face.

"Fast-food" relationships bypass investment in long-term friendships. As much as I have tried to immerse my children in the world of books and the arts and shield them from excessive technology, I cannot quarantine them. I observed one day that my son was playing an online checkers game with his friend, Michael, who lives up the street. I said, "We have a checkers game. Let's invite Michael over and you two can play in person." "It's much better on the computer, Mom," my son responded.

My teenage daughter, an excellent high school student, keeps such a busy schedule that she would rather listen to audio books than read them. Or, better yet, has the book been made into a movie?

My husband and I were discussing the library system one day. (He knows that libraries are my favorite retreats.) He mentioned that someday we wouldn't need libraries in our country. Every piece of reading material would be available by computer. I defended my natural habitat, "That will never happen. No one is going to curl up by a fire with a computer screen to read a book."

"That has already happened. Have you flown on a plane lately? You are out of touch with reality. With each younger generation, fewer books are being read," disclosed my husband. He is aware that I am a technological dinosaur. As a writer, I already know that publishers need to make a profit and they will not create products which do not sell. Their markets have changed.

Birkerts wants parents to know that we are embroiled in a battle for literacy. The experience of passionate reading, complete absorption in a book as a safe retreat from a hostile world, is becoming rare. Written communication, beyond e-mails and instant messaging, is becoming antiquated. He has observed that young people today quickly assimilate information but have lost depth of thinking. They know facts but have not gained wisdom.

In *Eats, Shoots & Leaves*, Lynne Truss discusses the impact of the electronic age on writing skills and the proper use of punctuation. She states: *The effect on language of the electronic age is obvious to all, even though the process has only just begun, and its ultimate impact is as yet unimaginable.*

In reading *First Mothers* by Bonnie Angelo, I was fascinated to observe one common thread running through the presidents' childhoods. Each young man was a voracious reader, saturated with books. Jimmy Carter's family actually grew up reading books at the dinner table. As they ate their meal together, each family member was engrossed in his or her own book. President Carter continued this tradition with his own children. *First Mothers* evidences the link between strong leadership and an immersion in literature.

Grappling with challenging reading material requires an investment of time, another precious commodity in our culture. "Fast-food" reading is preferred over nutritious books that can be savored over time. Deep reading is an acquired skill which requires practice. As a college professor of literature, Birkerts observes that with each year fewer of his students have acquired this skill, nor do they want to invest the time.

Do your children enjoy reading the Bible? If not, you may have diagnosed their lack of interest as a spiritual problem, when it is actually a literacy challenge. Fluent literacy is not simply the ability to read words, but a passionate love for the written word.

Readers are leaving the book as churchgoers have been leaving the church—because they no longer feel the need of what is to be gotten there.

Sven Birkerts

More Screen Time?

Our children are being raised by appliances.
Bill Moyers

A study released in 2005 by the Henry J. Kaiser Family Foundation revealed that children and teens spend an average of six and a half hours a day involved in media-related activities. Sixty-eight percent of the children surveyed had televisions in their bedrooms. Today's young people have been labeled the "plugged-in generation."

Children are by nature curious, active, inquisitive, and playful creatures. They drive us nuts as toddlers, touching and exploring everything, pushing every button, opening every cupboard, and wanting to "do it themselves." When these same bright children regularly choose passive behavior (observing others) vs. active, engaged behavior ("I want to try that"), something is wrong. Dr. Gary Krane writes in *Simple Fun for Busy People*:

> *It's no secret that most adults and much of our youth today have simply forgotten how to play, and accept sitting in front of a screen watching others joke and play and be challenged, as "play." This is distraction, not play. And we are living in the "over-distracted society," numbed by the TV drug. Our society has elevated distraction to an art form.*

In *Failure to Connect*, psychologist Jane Healy states that young, pre-literate children should not have access to computers. Her research shows that screen overload disrupts normal brain development. The American Academy of Pediatrics recommends that infants and toddlers not watch any television, because physical interaction is critical to brain development during the first two years of life.

Yet computer software is designed for infants as young as six months old; millions of Baby Einstein videos sell each year, and the national study "Zero to Six: Electronic Media in the Lives of Infants" found that a quarter of children under two years have televisions in their bedrooms. Two-thirds of the toddlers studied used screen media for an average of two hours daily, much more time than they spent engaged in books.

John Rosemond, family psychologist, believes that overexposure to television does not cause attention deficit disorder but can contribute to it. He advises that children not be permitted to watch television until they are fully literate. Obesity and health problems are other concerns for sedentary children who spend too much time watching screens, eating junk food, and avoiding outdoor activities.

When kids were once shooting baskets after school, now they're shooting bad guys in video games.

Mike Burita

Our local elementary school is constantly raising money to sustain a state-of-the-art computer lab. At the same time, the piano in the multipurpose room has fallen apart and will not be replaced, music and art programs are minimal, and teachers are strapped for textbooks and supplies. Why are we investing in more screen time for our children?

It is no longer the case that machines are an extension of our needs. On the contrary, we are extensions of the imperatives of machines.

Chuck Leddy

Frank McCourt, author of *Angela's Ashes*, described his destitute childhood as miserable. He didn't have access to books, so he came to appreciate how precious they were and considered the library a "feast." Neither did McCourt have access to television, radio, stereos, or even electric lighting. He explains: "So we told each other stories. We did our own singing; everybody sang. We didn't go around with headphones clamped to our ears."

Do today's children spend hours telling each other stories? Future writers begin as storytellers.

Storytelling is fundamental to the human search for meaning.

Mary Catherine Bateson

The #1 Family Ritual

I've often wondered what homing instinct leads us back to the table when events in our lives go awry. Perhaps it's the place where we feel the most grounded, and where we derive the most strength. Or maybe it's something more basic than that. Because sooner or later, we always get hungry. No matter what happens, we still need to eat. Family meals...anchor the day.

Doris Christopher
Come to the Table

Researchers on every front, Christian and secular, agree that regularly eating meals together is the most important ritual a family can observe. No matter what different directions we are running in, everyone still gets hungry and needs to eat. We can capitalize on this fact as parents. It is relatively unimportant what we eat as long as we sit to eat it together, discussing the day. "Talk is the foundation of a child's learning life," states Lucy Calkins. Screen time should be completely off-limits during meal times.

I am ferocious about this ritual, and my children never fail to remind me that this habit is outdated, "We don't know anyone else who eats dinner together." (These are also the same children who walk in late from a school event to discover the rest of our family eating dinner and cry, "What! You started dinner without me?!") The crazier our schedules are, the more we need to reconnect as family.

When I was growing up, the phone never rang during the dinner hour. No one dared interrupt meal time. Today the question is, "What dinner hour?" While our family eats, our main line rings, our daughters' phones ring, and multiple cell phones ring—often all at the same time. We do not answer them (thank goodness for voice mail). My husband, an avid sports fan, does not watch television sports events during dinner, and I am grateful to him that he gives our kids his full attention.

My husband and I also take the unpopular stand of not being available for night meetings unless they are absolutely necessary. Otherwise, we could attend a different meeting every night. I find especially humorous the parenting seminars that are offered on weeknights, such as "Strengthening Family Ties," "Helping Your Kids with Homework," or "Improving Communication with your Teen," requiring parents to leave their children at home to attend.

Mary Pipher calls for parents to build walls around one's family to protect it from cultural assault. She says that it is critical to set rituals when children are young to sustain them through the turbulent teen years.

I recently read in our local newspaper about two mothers being honored as "Soccer Moms of the Year." These exceptional women had driven thirty to forty hours a week, transporting their children to soccer practices, games, and weekend tournaments. They were on the road seven days a week. I could only wonder when was the last time their families enjoyed a meal together.

Smorgasbord Kids

In our sincere efforts to provide our children with every imaginable opportunity to become well-rounded, we are creating "smorgasbord kids." They attend dance classes, music lessons, baseball and soccer games, and sample endless activities. Parents negotiate weekly with coaches and teachers, juggling conflicting schedules, trying to fit it all in. We are raising multi-skilled, exhausted kids who never have enough time to breathe, much less play, read for pleasure, write in a journal, daydream, or brainstorm.

We are also raising kids who have general skills in a variety of areas but not one expert skill. As a music teacher, I know that it is impossible to excel on an instrument without hours of daily practice and focused dedication. You cannot have it both ways. Many young people vacillate between two behavior modes: overly structured activity or mind-numbing screen entertainment. This leaves little time for self-initiated creativity.

In reading the biographies of authors who experienced childhood before the technological era, I learned that these writers considered their greatest asset to be the opportunities they had as children to develop their imaginations. Having hours of free time forced them to find creative ways to fight boredom. They worked on homemade inventions, wrote plays and performed them in their garage, developed neighborhood newspapers, wrote stories, and immersed themselves in imaginative play.

Will future generations raised in our electronic culture be rich in artists?

Art is the signature of civilization.

Beverly Sills

Unexpected Lessons

Every year I learn one spiritual lesson from my garden. I didn't expect to learn any lessons this year because I didn't have time to plant. Surprisingly, God taught me the most profound lesson yet.

Come spring, I make my annual trip to the nursery and can't resist buying all kinds of seeds, bulbs, and plants. Intellectually I know I shouldn't do it, but I overplant all the pots on our deck. They are so full that nothing flourishes and everything fights to survive. Due to our travel schedule this summer, I never made my yearly trip to the nursery. I knew that I wouldn't be home to water and take care of the plants as needed.

I expected a bleak garden. Then the seeds I planted a year ago, that never had a chance last summer, began to sprout. In each pot, one seed bloomed into a beautiful plant that filled the container. Shocked, I realized that this fact of nature was true in our gardens, our personal lives, and our children's lives. As adults, we realize that when we are involved in too many activities, we are usually not doing anything well. The dilemma is that our children have learned this behavior from our modeling.

When our lives are overcrowded, nothing takes root and flourishes; but if we plant one seed, and give it room and time to grow, the results can be spectacular. But it requires patience and self-control.

An effective parent will not allow a TV or computer in a child's room. This is a dangerous world, and the danger is now inside the house. The exploiters want your kids. You must look out for them. Fight hard.

Bill O'Reilly

Reality Check

The reality is that my teenage children do watch television, play video games, instant message their friends, and use e-mail to communicate. We enjoy watching movies as a family. I want my teenagers to be comfortable with their culture, the technological age, and have healthy relationships with peers. Isolation is not the answer. The key is learning balance. My children did not have these screen privileges until they reached their teen years, and certain limits were applied. As young children, they read books for hours each day, enjoyed extensive play time, and had minimal television exposure.

As teens, my children never engage in screen activities behind closed doors. I am available to supervise them. As long as they continue to be physically active, excel at their academic and music studies, and spend time with our family, they may have limited access to screen activities. Setting reasonable guidelines and teaching teens to manage their time is a positive approach to our technological age.

Technology in itself is not evil, just as food is not evil. The abuse of technology and addictive behaviors are dangerous. Many activities in our culture can be beneficial in moderation. Our job as parents is to model a balanced lifestyle for our children.

Questions for Reflection

How have you and your family incorporated our electronic culture into your lives?

Do you control technology or does it control you?

Writing is the art of a listening heart.
　　　　　　　　　　　　Julia Cameron

Writing and reading decrease our sense of isolation.
They deepen and widen and expand our sense of life;
they feed the soul.
　　　　　　　　　　　　Anne Lamott

Families who treasure their traditions and rituals seem
automatically to have a sense of family. Traditions are
the underpinning in such families, regarded as necessities
not frills.
　　　　　　　　　　　　Dolores Curran

Section VI

Celebrating
with Writing

Chapter 17

Weaving Writing and Arts Traditions into Daily Life

The best writing activities do not involve pen and paper.
Peggy Kaye

Writing celebrations and relational activities can be integrated into daily life. Our goal is to create fun activities which celebrate writing, reading, the arts, and communication, understanding how important rituals are to family life. These activities should feel natural and playful, never forced or stressful. Too much structure can rob us of joy. This is not the time to correct spelling or grammar.

Family discussion is a vital part of brainstorming and sharing ideas, sometimes the best platform for writing, especially for young children. Meal times (often dinner) are the most opportune time to connect as a family and process the events of the day.

Dinner Table Games

When our children were young, one of our favorite dinner table games was "How was your day?" We wrote questions on slips of papers and placed them in a jar, adding to them through the years. Rotating around the table, we answered different questions, such as:

—What made you feel happy today?

—When did you feel grumpy today?

—When were you most frustrated today?

—What was your most embarrassing moment today?

—When did you laugh the most today?

—When were you silly today?

—What is the most important thing you learned today?

—How did God take care of you in a special way today?

Specific questions posed as a game encouraged specific answers. Simply asking our children, "How was your day?" would have yielded one word answers: "Fine" or "OK." We also kept a Blessings Box, from which our children could select the dinner blessing. Included were songs, Scripture verses, poems, well-known blessings, or their own written creations.

On Sunday evenings, our children would write down their favorite activities on slips of paper and put them in the Special Treat Jar. After dinner, our children would pull out one piece of paper, selecting the evening's activity, which might be a game, special snack, sing-along, or other activity. We kept a separate Surprise Jar which they added ideas to throughout the month. We selected one activity from the Surprise Jar on Saturdays, which was usually a fun outing for our family.

This way, the act of writing becomes associated with pleasurable moments and children learn to participate in family life through using the pen.

Ideas I have gleaned from other families follow:

—Similar to restaurants which use butcher paper as tablecloths to encourage business clients to brainstorm during lunch, one family covered their dining table with butcher paper. Throughout their meals, family members would draw or write ideas with marking pens to augment discussions.

—One family used white sheets as tablecloths during holiday dinners for extended family to write on. Each family member was encouraged to contribute a fun remembrance to the holiday cloth. In the years to follow, the special tablecloth of a specific holiday would reappear and additions could be made. This family had a collection of holiday tablecloths: one each for Valentine's Day, Easter,

Thanksgiving, Christmas, and others. As this family's children grew, notes from deceased relatives were especially meaningful.

—Another family created the Dessert Box. Family members wrote notes of thanks, appreciation, and admiration to one another throughout the month and put them in the Dessert Box. At the end of the month, they enjoyed a different kind of dessert, as they shared these "hugs on paper."

—One family played three-minute writing games at meal times. An egg timer was set and family members were encouraged to write three-minute poems about their day. Reading the poems made for fun table discussions. Sometimes family members would write three-minute postcards to friends or relatives.

—When dining in restaurants, one family enjoyed leaving encouraging notes of thanks for their servers. They began a practice of leaving notes for strangers in a variety of public places, hoping to brighten someone's day.

More Ideas

For more fun ideas, read Peggy Kaye's *Games for Writing.* Some of my favorite activities from her book include:

1) The domino game—As players throw the dice, writers script according to the number showing on the domino. For example, if the number four is thrown, players write four words or four sentences. This game is a fun way to explore poetry.

2) Alphabet books or lists—Using the alphabet as a guide, writers can create picture books or creative lists, selecting topics starting with each letter of the alphabet. Topics can include animals, pizza toppings, ice cream flavors, and more.

3) The writing treasure hunt—Words and sentences from a story are hidden throughout a house or yard. As players find parts of the story, they try to put them together. The player who completes the story first wins the game.

4) Word play—Young children can be encouraged to "write" words with dough, popcorn, Cheerios, jelly beans, M&M candies, or other fun items. Then they can eat their words!

For a variety of family games, consult Gary Krane's *Simple Fun For Busy People*. His "Alphabetical Kvetch" game is perfect for a bad day. Family members offer a complaint starting with each letter of the alphabet. Whoever finishes the list first (A–Z) wins the game. As you can imagine, by the end of the game, laughter has replaced a grumpy mood and improved a bad situation.

In contrast, Krane's "Three Best Things" game encourages players to list the three best things that happened to them during the day. Many of his ideas are ideal to incorporate with meal times.

The above alphabet games remind me of our family's favorite vacation game which we played while riding in the car. Players would rotate through letters of the alphabet, listing items to be brought on a trip. The hard part was listing all the previous items in order before adding the new item. This was a fun word game as well as a memory challenge. This game can be adapted for any topic.

Bedtime Rituals

While meal times are usually the best time to bond as a family, bedtime is the ideal time to focus on one-to-one relationships with each of your children. This process has been called "letting go of the day." Children share concerns and thoughts as they prepare for sleep that they normally do not share during the busy day. In addition to praying together and reading the Bible, here are some of our other favorite activities:

—When our children were young, I began the practice of "Truce Time." Before we prayed, I told them that they could share anything with me, good or bad (if they were angry or sad), with the promise that I would not judge, correct, or instruct them. I would simply listen and keep their concerns completely confidential. I wanted them to learn to talk to God with the same freedom, bringing closure to the day. I also wanted them to never "let the sun go down on [their] anger." My children misunderstood the word "truce" and called it "trust time." I realized that this was a better term and even today my young adult children will say, "This is trust time stuff, Mom."

—We also created family songs to be sung at bedtime, with biblical concepts we were studying. We would set our own words to familiar tunes.

—One well-known bedtime ritual that we included was "one grateful, one grumble." I encouraged our children to pray to God, sharing something that they were grateful for and something that they were upset about, teaching the concepts of thankfulness and petition.

—We enjoyed telling round-robin stories. Often our children would gather in one bed to read books, and then we would create our own story, each telling a different part as we rotated it between us. We enjoyed leaving the story at a cliff hanging point as we passed it on to the next storyteller. When our children were tired, they asked me to tell the entire story, using their names given to characters doing outrageous things.

—While we read a variety of books throughout the day, we read holiday books at bedtime. Through the years, we collected a set of books for each holiday.

—For tactile learners, writing on a child's back with your finger is a fun way to communicate, as he or she tries to guess the words. This is also a soothing activity.

—With a little creativity, the act of tucking a child into bed can be especially fun. As you jump around on the bed and move the covers up and down, your child can be a letter being tucked into an envelope, mailed in a mailbox, and sent through the city to the recipient. Your child can be an airplane taking off on a runway, flying through the air, and landing. Your child will enjoy brainstorming the possibilities.

—Some adults and children keep a bedtime journal, flashlight, and pen next to their beds to jot down thoughts that come to them late at night or in the middle of the night, whether it's an idea or a flash of insight they don't want to forget.

While not all the ideas found in this section and throughout the chapter are pen-to-paper writing activities, remember that family sharing, story creation, reading, and communication are the foundation for sharing on paper, with the ultimate goal being healthy relationships.

Creating Your Own Family Holidays

Our phone rang at 10:00 p.m. The mother of my young son's best friend said, "Help! My son is putting his shoes outside his bedroom door for St. Nick's Day. He told me that they will be filled with treats tomorrow morning to start the Christmas season. What is he talking about?" I profusely apologized.

One of my children had again assumed that the entire world celebrated the silly holidays that we did and that other mothers were as crazy as I was. As our children grew, we celebrated a myriad of holidays unique to our family, such as Stone Soup Day, Winnie the Pooh Day, half-birthdays, St. Lucia Day, Harvest Home, spiritual birthdays, Mozart's birthday tea, and more. Our goal was to celebrate at least one holiday (family ritual) a week. Creating a calendar of these mini holidays took years to evolve. Our children enjoyed participating in the planning process. We were certainly enjoying family bonding experiences.

Sometimes we ended up celebrating a different holiday almost every night or a combination on the same day, laughing that we couldn't keep them straight. For example, did you know that January 27 is the birthday of Amadeus Mozart, Lewis Carroll, and Thomas Crapper? We celebrated Mozart's birthday with a tea party while listening to his music, and discussed *Alice in Wonderland*. Yet my son's favorite part of the celebration was remembering that Thomas Crapper invented the toilet.

I have simply enjoyed collecting holiday rituals through the years. If you are thinking that I am completely nuts, please bypass this chapter. But if you would like to create your own family calendar of mini-holiday celebrations, read on. The key is to not copy another family's celebrations but to develop your own unique rituals, based on your distinct interests and experiences. You are creating a special family identity that cannot be duplicated. Including your children in the planning stages is critical. In the following pages, you will explore a cornucopia of ideas that you can adapt to your own family. I invite you to pick and choose the celebrations which will be most meaningful for your family. You may want to complete your own research at the library or online, pursuing your individual interests.

Authors' Birthdays

Honoring authors on their birthdays is a fun way to celebrate literature. Your children will develop a preference for certain authors through the years, depending on their ages. They will enjoy planning birthday parties for their favorite authors, reading passages, and using themes from their books. If you are celebrating Patricia Polacco, you can make the cake from her book, *Thundercake*. If you are celebrating Jack Prelutsky, you can read a variety of his poems. When we celebrated A. A. Milne's birthday and his Winnie the Pooh books, we dined on dishes made with honey and had a tea party with all my children's favorite stuffed bears. Clues from your favorite authors' books will inspire limitless celebrations. I have included serious authors as well as some of our favorite authors of children's books. As your children age, they will be introduced to more serious literature. Here are some examples for each month:

January	3	J. R. R. Tolkien
	4	Jakob Grimm
	12	Jack London
	18	A. A. Milne—National Pooh Day
	27	Lewis Carroll
February	7	Charles Dickens
		Laura Ingalls Wilder
	8	Jules Verne
	27	Henry Longfellow
		John Steinbeck
March	26	Robert Frost
April	2	Hans Christian Andersen
	21	Charlotte Bronte

	23	William Shakespeare
May	15	L. Frank Baum
	22	Sir Arthur Conan Doyle
June	2	Norton Juster
July	4	Nathaniel Hawthorne
	11	E. B. White
	12	Henry David Thoreau
	21	Ernest Hemingway
	28	Beatrix Potter
August	1	Herman Melville
	6	Alfred Lord Tennyson
	20	Emily Bronte
September	11	O. Henry
	25	William Faulkner
October	31	Katherine Paterson
November	1	Stephen Crane
	13	Robert Louis Stevenson
	24	Frances Hodgson Burnett
	28	John Bunyan
	29	Louisa May Alcott
		Madeleine L'Engle
		C. S. Lewis
	30	Mark Twain
December	10	Emily Dickinson
	16	Jane Austen
	30	Rudyard Kipling

When my children were young, some of their other favorite authors (with corresponding birthdays) were:

March	2	Dr. Seuss
	20	Louis Sachar

April	12	Beverly Cleary
May	23	Margaret Wise Brown
June	10	Maurice Sendak
	18	Chris Van Allsburg
	25	Eric Carle
July	11	Patricia Polacco
		James Stevenson
September	8	Jack Prelutsky
	13	Roald Dahl
	15	Tomie dePaola
	25	Shel Silverstein
October	10	James Marshall
	26	Steven Kellogg
November	25	Marc Brown
December	1	Jan Brett
	20	Mercer Mayer

For more biographical information about authors, you can consult the *Contemporary Author* series (adult literature) or *Something About the Author* series (children's literature). These can be found in the reference section of your library. Many authors also have websites.

Book Celebrations

You can use favorite books as inspiration for meals. In the fall, our family reads *Stone Soup* at the dinner table and we eat our version of Stone Soup. One year we found a book at the library entitled *Mother Grumpy's Cookies* (author unknown), which inspired us to make cookies or other sweets whenever we felt grumpy.

We also have a large collection of books for each season and holiday. My children enjoyed rediscovering these books every year as we brought them out to place in the holiday basket. In addition to several series such as Marc Brown's holiday books, Jack Prelutsky's holiday poem books, and the Cranberry series by Wende and Harry Devlin, we have enjoyed reading *The Country Bunny and the Little Gold Shoes* by DuBose Heyward and Patricia Polacco's *Chicken Sunday* during the Easter season. *The Tale of Three Trees* by Angela Elwell Hunt is appropriate for Easter or Christmas, providing a nice introduction to reading scriptural accounts.

Sharing the titles of all our favorite holiday books is beyond the scope of this book. For more ideas, consult a librarian or try to purchase one book per holiday each year, starting when your children are young. This is how our collection grew. I look forward to someday sharing these books with my grandchildren when they visit.

Famous Artists' Birthdays

Understanding that the arts are intertwined, celebrate the world of music, art, dance, and theater, in addition to celebrating literature. Listen to the music of famous composers on their birthdays, visit art museums, attend the ballet and other theater productions. Attend a play by Shakespeare on his birthday or a concert featuring the works of Beethoven on his birthday. If you are unable to plan trips, you can check out music recordings, books of art work, or videos of famous productions at your local library.

Some examples are:

January	27	Mozart
	31	Schubert
February	3	Mendelssohn
	7	Ballet Day
	23	Handel
	25	Renoir
March	1	Chopin
	4	Vivaldi
	6	Michelangelo

	7	Ravel
	21	Johann Sebastian Bach
	21	National Dance Day
	25	Bartok
	30	Van Gogh
	31	Haydn
April	15	DaVinci
	23	Prokofiev
May	7	Tchaikovsky, Brahms
	11	Martha Graham—Modern Dance
	22	Wagner
	25	National Tap Dance Day
June	8	Schumann
	11	R. Strauss
	17	Stravinsky
July	15	Rembrandt
August	22	Debussy
September	8	Dvorak
	26	George Gershwin
October	10	Verdi
	22	Liszt
	25	Picasso
November	6	John Philip Sousa
	14	Monet
		Copland
	24	Scott Joplin
December	11	Berlioz
	16	Beethoven

More Famous Birthdays

Your child may be fascinated with sports figures, famous scientists, or other historical figures. Use their interests to encourage them to research the lives of famous people who have made contributions to our world. Note their birth dates. You can celebrate these birthdays by writing biographies or creating mock interviews in a talk show format. Go to a ball game. Visit a science museum, try an experiment, or create your own invention. Visit an observatory. View historical exhibits. Each of these activities can become fun annual events.

Here are some examples to start your own list:

January	4	Louis Braille
	17	Benjamin Franklin
February	4	Rosa Lee Parks—Take a Stand for What You Believe In Celebration
	6	Babe Ruth
	11	Thomas Edison—National Inventors Day
	15	Susan B. Anthony
March	3	Alexander Graham Bell
	10	Harriet Tubman
	14	Albert Einstein
	24	Harry Houdini
May	12	Florence Nightingale
June	8	Frank Lloyd Wright
	11	Jacques Cousteau
	27	Helen Keller—This is Deaf/Blindness Awareness Week.
July	24	Amelia Earhart
	30	Henry Ford
August	19	Orville Wright—National Aviation Day
	27	Mother Teresa
September	24	Jim Henson—Muppets Day

November	10	Martin Luther
	26	Charles Schultz
December	5	Walt Disney

For more ideas, consult the *Current Biography* series or *the National American Biography* series in the reference section of your library. For information about scientists, consult *Scientists: The Lives and Works of 150 Scientists*, edited by P. Saari and S. Allison.

Biblical Themes

You can celebrate your favorite biblical figures by reading relevant passages of Scripture. Many of us identify with specific biblical characters. You can celebrate verses or books of the Bible which have been especially meaningful in your life. You can incorporate Old and New Testament rituals into your family plans. Some families celebrate the Purim Feast in February; others celebrate the Passover supper. Pentecost can be remembered at the end of May. For some of the holidays listed in this chapter, you can select Scripture verses as themes. For example, read Scriptures about the Holy Spirit during May to celebrate Pentecost, or read verses about encouragement in honor of Be An Encourager Day. See BiblicalHolidays.com for information on the Bible holidays.

Special Days for Family Members

Being singled out and honored for exactly who one is is one of the ultimate joys of life.

Meg Cox

In addition to celebrating the birthdays of famous people, you can also celebrate mini-birthdays for your own family members. While some people find the acknowledgement of birthdays to be frivolous and unnecessary, others understand that birthdays give us a concrete opportunity to honor and remember individuals, to make them feel special, not based on their performance but simply on who they are. We take the time to communicate in tangible ways that family members are loved and treasured. Here are some ideas for mini-birthday celebrations:

—I wanted each of our children to have a special day each month to feel honored. I chose their birth date. For example, if your child was born on March 5, you can celebrate him or her on the fifth of every month. The day began with a candle on my children's breakfast plate. We would sing the Disney© song, "A Very Merry Unbirthday to You©." I would serve their favorite foods, give them silly presents, and plan other special treats. They were "King or Queen for a Day" and learned to honor their siblings on their respective days.

—Half-birthdays were fun, as we made half-cakes and half-cards. My husband enjoyed singing only half the birthday song. Sometimes we would create acrostics based on our children's names, listing one of their special qualities for each letter of their name. Each family member would read his or her acrostic. An example would be:

JOHN   **J**oyful
                    Observant
                    Helpful
                    Noble

—Treasure hunts are fun adventures for half or annual birthdays. Family members can create elaborate hunts, leaving poem clues throughout the house and yard as the guest of honor searches for a birthday surprise.

—Birthdays posters are fun ways to remember landmark birthdays. On our children's first birthdays as well as their first double digit birthday (ten years), guests signed a birthday poster with wishes for the future. These are lifetime keepsakes, recording messages from friends who have been significant through the years.

—Spiritual birthdays are a more serious day of honor. I have told my children that remembering the day they committed their lives to Jesus Christ is a more important event than their chronological birthday. The date that one was baptized often is a natural day to celebrate one's spiritual birthday. As our children have left for college, I have tried to send regular care packages in remembrance of all our crazy holidays but this is the most important package that I send. In remembering their spiritual birthdays, I hope to send gifts of spiritual encouragement and remind them of their faith in the midst of their busy schedules.

—Star birthdays refer to that special birthday which occurs on the date of one's age. For example, if one turns fifteen years of age on August 15, August 15 is his or her Star Birthday.

—Celebrate birthday buddies. You may have family members who share birthdays on the same day or during the same week. My daughter was born three hours after my husband's birthday. They are birthday buddies. In one family I know, the mother and daughter share the same birth date.

—Acknowledging Birthday Eve is fun, as the birthday girl or boy prepares to turn a year older, with new responsibilities and privileges.

Heritage Days

Research the roots of your ancestors to incorporate traditions of foreign countries when appropriate. For example, my husband's family originally came from Germany. We celebrate Oktoberfest during the week of my husband's October birthday. His favorite meal is sauerbraten. My mother immigrated to the United States from Mexico as a young woman. When our children were young, we celebrated a version of Las Posadas, going from room to room in our home, seeking room at the inn. My oldest daughter was born on September 16, Mexican Independence Day, which was a fun remembrance of her heritage on her birthday. Your family will enjoy learning about the traditions of their ancestors.

One friend did not have French roots but her children were studying French, so her family celebrated Bastille Day by making crepes for breakfast. If you enjoy adding an international flair to your family events, you can celebrate a different country every month.

Research the history of your state and discover the date of your state's Admission Day. Make special foods in honor of your state's birthday (e.g., sourdough bread for Alaska, potato dishes for Idaho, and more). You can celebrate the Admission Day of other states that you have vacationed in or have relatives residing in.

When our children were young, we had close friends who were missionaries in China so we enjoyed celebrating Chinese New Year.

Writing and Reading Celebrations

A variety of national holidays give us the opportunity to celebrate literacy in various ways:

January is International Creativity Month
First week in January—Letter Writing Week
January 2—Science Fiction Day
Second week in January—International Thank You Days
January 23—John Hancock's Birthday—National Handwriting Day

February is Library Lovers' Month
First week in February—Children's Authors and Illustrators Week
Second week in February—Freelance Writers' Appreciation Week

First week in March—National Write a Letter of Appreciation Week
March 2—Read Across America Day in honor of Dr. Seuss' birthday

April is National Poetry Month
April 2—International Children's Book Day
April 11—Write Your Memoirs Day
Second week in April—Young People's Poetry Week
Fourth week—Family Reading Week
April 28—Poetry Day

May is National Book Month
First week in May—Pen-Friends Week
      National Postcard Week
      Reading is Fun Week
May 1—Mother Goose Day
May 5—Cartoonist's Day

May 16—Biographer's Day
May 30—First U.S. newspaper was published.

August is May Your Reading Be a Haven Month
August 22—National Punctuation Day

September is Be Kind to Editors and Writers Month
September 6—Read a Book Day
September 8—United Nations International Literacy Day
September 22—Dear Diary Day

October 16—Daniel Webster's Birthday and Dictionary Day
Third week in October—Teen Read Week

November is Family Stories Month
First week in November —Children's Book Week
November 1—National Author's Day
November 9—National Young Reader's Day

December 1—Becky Thatcher Day, in honor of girls who have written or inspired literature.

Fun Food Holidays

Some families find cooking together to be the best way to spend time with one another. Children work on literacy skills through reading recipes, writing recipes, creating family cookbooks, and planning menus and parties. Here are some fun national holidays to inspire your culinary explorations:

January is Hot Tea Month, Soup Month, and Oatmeal Month
January 23—Pie Day

February is Bake for Family Fun Month and National Cherry Month
The third week in February —National Pancake Week
The third week in March —Chocolate Week

March 15—Pasta Day in Italy

May is Eat Dessert First Month, Strawberry Month, and National
     Barbecue Month
The first week in May —Muffin Week and Raisin Week

June is National Candy Month
June 4—Donut Day
June 9—National Taco Day
June 18—Picnic Day

July is National Culinary Arts Month, National Hot Dog Month, and
     Blueberries Month
The fourth week in July — National Salad Week
July 18—National Ice Cream Day

August is National Sandwich Month
August 22—National Hamburger Day

September is National Biscuit Month, National Honey Month,
       National Potato Month, and National Rice Month
The first week in September —National Waffle Week
September 13—Fortune Cookie Day
September 22—The Ice Cream Cone's Birthday

October is Peanuts Month, National Chili Month, National Cookie
     Month, National Popcorn Month, and National Pizza
     Month

November is Peanut Butter Lover's Month
November 3—Sandwich Day and the birthday of Earl Montague who
     invented it
November 17—Homemade Bread Day
November 21—Pumpkin Pie Day

The first week in December —Cookie Cutter Week
December 12 —Gingerbread House Day

Even More Holidays

You are learning that that you can celebrate ANYTHING. The more unique the idea, the better. You can celebrate your pets' birthdays. You can remember the day you moved into your house and celebrate your home's birthday. Since we moved into our home in October many years ago, we combine our home's birthday with Harvest Home, a celebration of harvest and thankfulness to God for His blessings and provision.

Here are some more unique holidays:

January	3	Sip Day—drinking straw patented
	16	Religious Freedom Day
	21	National Hugging Day
	28	Backwards Day
	29	Puzzle Day
	31	Inspire Your Heart with Art Day
February		National Friendship Month
		Wild Bird Feeding Month
	1	Robinson Crusoe Day
		Be An Encourager Day
	2	Groundhog Day
	6	Pay A Compliment Day
	8	Smile Day
	11	National Shut-In Visitation Day
	14	Have A Heart Day (in honor of American Heart Month, to fight heart disease)
March		Youth Art Month
	4	International Scrapbooking Day
	7	Monopoly Game Anniversary
	10	Learn What Your Name Means Day
	20	National Quilting Day
	21	Flower Day
	26	Make Up Your Own Holiday
	28	Patty Smith Hill's Birthday (composer of "Happy Birthday To You")
April		National Kite Month

National Garden Month
First week—Golden Rule Week and National
    Week Of The Ocean
Third week—Astronomy and Heritage Week

10	National Siblings Day
11	Barbershop Quartet Day
17	Husband Appreciation Day
24	Astronomy Day
30	Arbor Day

May

National Family Month
National Bike Month
First week—National Wildflower Week (in honor
    of May Day)
National Hug Week
Be Kind To Animals Week
Third week—National New Friends, Old Friends
    Week
Fourth week—National Backyard Games Week

2	Sibling Appreciation Day
4	Relationship Renewal Day
18	Visit Your Relatives Day
	International Museum Day

June

Effective Communication Month
Sports America Kids Month
Rose Month
First week—International Volunteers Week and
    Pet Appreciation Week

5	National Yoyo Day
14	Family History Day
18	World Juggling Day and National Splurge Day
22	National Forgiveness Day
24	Celebration Of The Senses Day
26	Celebrate Your Marriage Day

July

1	First U.S. Zoo Anniversary

7	Father And Daughter Take A Walk Day
10	Teddy Bear Picnic Day
11	Cheer Up The Lonely Day
15	Christmas In July—Clement Moore's Birthday
17	Birthday Of Disneyland© (1955)

August
National Inventors' Month
First Week—National Smile Week

1	Sister/Brother Friendship Day
12	Family Day
13	Middle Child Day and Left Hander Day
15	National Relaxation Day
17	Sandcastle Day
22	Be An Angel Day
25	Kiss And Make Up Day

September
National Sewing Month
Mindmapping and Brainstorming Month

10	Sew Be It! Day and Swap Ideas Day
	2nd Sunday in September—Grandparents' Day
18	Wife Appreciation Day
19	Women's Friendship Day
	Third Week—Religious Freedom Week
20	Eat Dinner As A Family Day
22	Hobbit Day
23	Checkers Day
25	Family Health And Fitness Day
26	National Good Neighbor Day and Johnny Appleseed's Birthday
27	Ancestor Appreciation Day
30	Gutenberg Bible Anniversary

October
Computer Learning Month
National Communicate With Your Kid Month
National Go On A Field Trip Month
Third week—National Character Counts Week

2	Snoopy's© Birthday (Anniversary of Peanuts comic strip)

6	Name Your Car Day
12	Scrabble© Day
19	Evaluate Your Life Day
23	Make A Difference Day
	Last Sunday—Reformation Sunday

November — I Am So Thankful Month
Cozy Cuddles For Kids Month (through mid-December)
First Week—Kids' Goal Setting Week
Fourth Week—National Bible Week
National Family Week
National Game And Puzzle Week

8	National Parents As Teachers Day
13	World Kindness Day
14	National American Teddy Bear Day
18	Mickey Mouse's© Birthday
21	World Hello Day

December

2	Red-Nosed Reindeer Day
5	National Communicate With Your Kids Day
	Bathtub Party Day
6	St. Nicholas Day
12	Poinsettia Day
13	St. Lucia Day
15	Mistletoe Day
16	Anniversary of the Boston Tea Party
18	Nutcracker Ballet first performed
21	Crossword Puzzle Day

Creating Your Calendar

In reality, how do you incorporate these ideas into weekly life? This process takes time and hopefully will involve your children's help. Obtain a large, blank calendar (without specific year references) and begin listing fun days that are important to your family. Today you may list two special family celebrations in January. Ten years from now, you may have ten mini celebrations in January.

Keep this calendar as your family reference calendar. You need not create a new one each year. You can transfer dates onto your personal yearly calendars. Dates that are not birthdays can change annually. Check a current almanac at your library or simply enjoy celebrating on approximate dates. Did my family celebrate all the listed holidays? No, of course not. We tried to pick at least one or two different celebrations a week depending on our schedule and interests. The goal was to set aside a special family time. Though hard to believe, the included dates are only a selection of famous birthdays and official holidays.

There are holidays as ridiculous as: Talk Like A Pirate Day, International Goof Off Day, National Open An Umbrella Indoors Day, Squirrel Appreciation Day, Sneak Some Zucchini Onto Your Neighbor's Porch Night, and others. Examples of more serious holidays are the anniversary of the Challenger Space Shuttle explosion, National Eating Disorders Awareness Week, and National Cancer Survivors Day.

In this chapter I tried to include holidays that were most conducive to creating relational family time. In the reference section of your library, you can find *Chase's Calendar of Events* (annually updated). Another excellent source is Holidays on the Net www.holidays.net. Holidays on the Net also updates their calendars each year. *The Independent Book of Anniversaries* by George Beal is helpful.

The real fun begins when your children realize the combination of mini holidays that are unique to your family. For example, my son's birthday corresponds with Earl Montague's birthday, the inventor of the sandwich which is celebrated as National Sandwich Day, and which encouraged fun sandwich creations when he was young. My younger daughter's birthday corresponded with the last week in October, so we annually gave her a Pumpkin Party. Guests came in costume and we had pumpkin hunts, similar to Easter egg hunts. Anny, a young girl from Haiti that we supported through an international children's organization for years, had her birthday on February 14. We sent her birthday gifts in honor of Valentine's Day (Sharing Love Day). While my oldest daughter's birthday fell on Mexican Independence Day, her half-birthday was on St. Patrick's Day, so we combined the celebrations.

Be creative and let your imagination run wild as you capitalize on overlapping holidays that fit your family identity.

"You are what you eat," as the saying goes. Similarly...you are what you celebrate.

Meg Cox

Questions for Reflection

How can you integrate literacy activities into your daily traditions? weekly traditions? monthly traditions? annual traditions?

Celebrations build walls around families.
Mary Pipher

If holiday occasions are celebrated in the right spirit, the glow from these days can spread out over the rest of life.
Bruno Bettelheim

Children who are bound by biological or legal ties can claim the title of family, but to actually be a family...requires a commitment to spending a good amount of time in the pursuit of nothing more than being together.
John Rosemond

Lack of time might be the most pervasive enemy the healthy family has.
Dolores Curran

Chapter 18

Weaving Literacy
into Annual Celebrations

Magical writing is contagious.
Lucy Calkins

We will close this section with discussing ways to integrate the family writing lifestyle and rituals with familiar holidays. If you are interested in this book, I would imagine that you already have your own set of special traditions for major holidays and family events. I will not attempt to duplicate those. The challenge is to celebrate traditional holidays without sacrificing the family focus of mini holidays. Look for new, creative ways to incorporate literacy activities, giving these celebrations a relational and spiritual focus vs. a commercial emphasis. These three ways may help your family enjoy approaching major holidays, give them purpose, and also lower your stress level as a parent:

1) Expand the holiday through the month, culminating in your traditional celebration.

2) Focus on biblical themes during holiday months, and on understanding the Christian roots of most holidays.

3) Encourage family members to exchange creative gifts of the heart. Keep the focus of every holiday centered on caring for people, reaching out to family, friends, and strangers.

"Keep Christ in Christmas" is a popular saying heard during the Christmas season, yet Christ can be the center of most holiday celebrations throughout the year.

Extending Holidays Throughout the Month

The best method I have found for avoiding a commercial holiday influence is celebrating a specific holiday theme in small doses on a daily basis throughout the month, instead of succumbing to a Hallmark© deadline. For example, February is the ideal month to celebrate a family's love.

On February 1 we select each other's names out of a jar. Each family member leaves love notes and small creative gifts for their "secret pal" in surprising places for two weeks. On Valentine's Day, we write love poems to our secret pals and give them a special final gift. Their job is to guess who we are. The guessing game is as much fun as the Valentine's Day festivities. February is a perfect time to read First Corinthians 13 and other verses about biblical love. Similar to the secret pal activity during February, St. Patrick's Day can be celebrated with leprechaun surprises left for family members during early March.

Celebrating the resurrection of our Lord Jesus Christ offers us an excellent opportunity to reread the different Gospel accounts with our family in the weeks before Easter. As we attend a Palm Sunday service, Maundy Thursday service, reenactment of the Passover supper, or Good Friday service during holy week, we are preparing for Easter Sunday. When young, my children also enjoyed bunny tea parties (with all their stuffed bunnies in attendance) and egg-coloring parties.

Some families observe Lent by giving up an activity (e.g., television viewing) to spend time focusing on their relationship with God. Other families add activities during Lent to focus on serving God, such as helping a neighbor or visiting older relatives.

The fall season is a natural time to practice thankfulness. Starting on November 1, our family members daily write what we are thankful for on slips of paper during the dinner hour and put them in the Thankful Jar. On Thanksgiving Eve, we read the contents of the jar and brainstorm our annual Thanksgiving acrostic. We record this acrostic in our holiday journal. Each letter of THANKSGIVING represents something specific our family was thankful for during the year.

Another favorite activity my children enjoyed was painting holiday sugar cookies during the week before a holiday. The paint consisted of heavy whipping cream with added food coloring. Using small paper cups made an assortment of paint colors possible. We had a collection of cookie cutters for each holiday: hearts for Valentine's Day, shamrocks for St. Patrick's Day, bunnies and crosses for Easter, pumpkins for October, turkeys for Thanksgiving, and a variety of shapes for Christmas.

As different holidays approach, think of ways to celebrate with a daily activity, including them in your family calendar. Avoid the "feast or famine" approach to holidays, where few or no activities are planned through the month and all the holiday festivities occur on one day. This can be overwhelming for young children, and the theme and purpose become lost. In small doses, holidays can be wonderful teaching tools.

Holiday Biblical Themes

Introduce your family to the Christian roots of different holidays. Read about the history of holidays and become familiar with the Christian meaning of symbols.

See BiblicalHolidays.com for a listing of the Biblical holiday dates. The site includes history, ideas, crafts, activities, articles, links, a list group, and information on each holiday observed in Bible times such as Sabbath, Passover, Unleavened Bread, Firstfruits, Pentecost, Trumpets (Rosh Hashanah), the Day of Atonement (Yom Kippur), and Tabernacles (Succoth), Hanukkah (Chanukah or the Feast of Dedication) and Purim. These Feasts days or Sabbaths are a beautiful picture of the Messiah's first and second coming.

Some holidays have pagan roots, but most have Christian influences. Focus on legends as a springboard for biblical discussions. Legends are not always fact but they inspire us with biblical ideals.

You can focus on a different biblical theme each month and these can change through the years. Read Scripture verses representative of the theme throughout the month.

Here are some ideas:

January—A New Creation in Christ
February—Loving One Another and Sacrificing For One Another
March—Mission Outreach
April—Christ's Resurrection
May—Pentecost, Holy Spirit
September or October—Harvest Home (Read Robert Munger's *My Heart, Christ's Home*)
November—Thankfulness to God
December—Christ's Birth

The theme for summer vacation months may be Paul's missionary journeys or the pilgrimages made by God's people in the Old Testament.

Gifts of the Heart

Celebrate caring for others with giving gifts from the heart. Engage in personal activities vs. purchasing activities. Creativity is the key to personalizing family celebrations, through composing poems or music, writing heartfelt letters, collecting flowers into a bouquet, making gifts or art work, hosting a meal, or baking someone's favorite dessert. Some families enjoy creating individualized coupon books for friends and family, with each coupon representing the gift of time and effort. Coupon offers may include a car wash, picnic lunch, back rub, or an afternoon of babysitting.

With every celebration, try to find ways to honor others through writing. For example, write letters of appreciation to parents on Mother's or Father's Day. Interview veterans, especially grandparents who served in the military, on Memorial Day or Veterans Day.

Giving a meaningful gift is not dependent on monetary resources. Learning to give to others in tangible ways is a learned skill, requiring practice.

Keeping Christ in Christmas

Ironically, many families find that during the Christmas celebration is their greatest challenge to focusing on Christ. Elaborate decorations, too many parties and activities, shopping trips, and an endless "to do list" all make for a stressful season, especially for mothers. Stressed mothers are less likely to have time for nurturing family activities and sacred moments. Simplifying Christmas and focusing on its true meaning can help families celebrate our Lord's birth in meaningful ways. The key is focusing on our relationship with Christ and giving to others, especially those who cannot give back to us. This can be done throughout the month of December, with daily spiritual reminders.

Lighting candles on the Advent wreath every Sunday or adding figures to a crèche scene are opportunities to have weekly devotions. When our children were young, we celebrated the holiday in small doses every evening after dinner. My children called it "Candle Time." We would sing one Christmas carol, read one Scripture verse, select one Christmas card from friends and pray for them, open chocolate Advent calendars, and write down a gift we gave to Jesus that day, putting the slip of paper in the Birthday Box. Gifts included kind words, thoughtful acts, letters sent, our participation in a church concert, donations made to organizations helping the homeless or other missions organizations, toys purchased for families in need, or other acts of compassion.

A few days before Christmas, we had a birthday party for Jesus, complete with birthday decorations, and read aloud all the gifts we had given Him during the month.

We tried to remember St. Lucia, a symbol of charity, during our Christmas festivities. In Scandinavia she was known as the Queen of Lights, rising early each morning to bake bread for starving people during a famine. Carrying a lantern, she would leave bread on doorsteps at dawn for those in need. The ruling class warned her to stop. She refused, staying faithful to God's calling, and was martyred. Today's custom is that the eldest daughter in a family, wearing a candle-lit wreath on her head, awakens her family with freshly baked goods. St. Lucia Day (December 13) represents the act of caring for others in need, which we can celebrate through personally delivering baked goods or sending donations to organizations which feed the homeless.

During one Christmas season, our eldest daughter, who was working as a student teacher in a local classroom, learned that her favorite student longed for a scooter. She knew that he would not be receiving gifts that year due to a precarious home environment. Unbeknownst to us, she purchased the scooter and delivered it to him on Christmas Eve. His ecstatic response was the best gift she received that year.

In the spirit of St. Lucia Day, Poinsettia Day (December 12) is an opportunity to deliver poinsettias to those who need some Christmas cheer. Mistletoe Day is on December 15. Mistletoe was originally a symbol of forgiveness. On Mistletoe Day, people embraced their enemies, offering and seeking forgiveness in anticipation of beginning a new year. The idea of the romantic kiss under the mistletoe came much later. This holiday is the ideal time for us to reconcile strained relationships and resolve conflicts, celebrating that Christ came to reconcile us with God.

In addition to daily and weekly observations of Christmas, you can plan annual traditional events for your family. Some families enjoy attending a sing-along Messiah concert or performance of the Nutcracker, or travel to the mountains to ski for a weekend. Others like to plan a tree trimming party and watch the movie, "White Christmas." We enjoyed playing a game called "Criss-Crossed Carols" while trimming the tree. Each family member would challenge another to sing the words of one Christmas song to the tune of another Christmas song. For example, one would be asked to sing the lyrics of "We Three Kings" to the tune "O Christmas Tree", or "Jolly Old St. Nicholas" lyrics to the tune "It Came Upon a Midnight Clear." The challenges would become more difficult as the game progressed.

The New Year—A New Beginning

New Year's Day provides us with a special opportunity to reflect on the past year and look forward to the coming year as a family. Our family created awards for the previous year for each family member, honoring significant achievements. We also each wrote down our best memory of the year and one specific goal for the coming year. We annually wrote these reflections in a holiday journal that can be read through the years. Especially fun was seeing if we accomplished our set goals on the following New Year's Day.

When our children were young, we held a New Year's Day poster contest. The children cut up the season's Christmas cards to create giant collages on poster board, seeing who could be the most creative. Of course, each child won a prize.

On New Year's Eve, one family I know draws a timeline in pictures of the past year, remembering the most important events. They review the past year and then write down prayers for each family member, including themselves. They seal them in envelopes and open them the following New Year's Eve, marveling at ways that God answered their prayers.

You may want to continue your Christmas celebration beyond December 25. The twelve days of Christmas actually begin on December 26 and continue to January 6, when we celebrate Twelfth Night, Epiphany. We can remember the Wise Men's arrival to worship Jesus by discussing what gifts we can bring to Jesus today. In some cultures, children put their shoes outside their bedroom door on January 5 to receive surprises from the Wise Men the next morning.

Simplifying Christmas, keeping the focus on Christ, and continuing the spirit of the holidays into January sets the tone for celebrating other holidays with a spiritual emphasis throughout the year.

An Ultimate Celebration: Rite of Passage

Hope chests were once popular gifts presented to young women who left home to marry. I received a hope chest from my husband's grandparents filled with precious linens and other treasures that I still use almost thirty years later. His grandparents are deceased but their legacy lives on in our home. My husband's grandmother was an artist and we have several of her paintings hanging throughout our house. His grandfather was a lighting gaffer for Paramount Pictures©. He sang duets during breaks with his friend, Bing Crosby. Every Christmas we bring out a Santa suit for one of us to wear on Christmas Eve, that is rumored to be from the costume collection of the movie *White Christmas©*.

Hope chests are no longer popular. Rarely do children live at home until they marry, and some choose to remain single. We need to find a different way to celebrate our children's passage into adulthood on a special day. You may choose as their adult marker the day they leave home, their twenty-first birthday, their first day of full-time employment, their wedding day, their college graduation day, or other significant event.

As your children age, start creating an emotional hope chest for them, not filled with linens and china, but filled with remembrances from their childhood and your tangible messages of love and support that you can give them upon their entrance into adulthood. Try to create a special gift that chronicles their life story. Their past is an anchor as they move into the future.

One mother sewed together all her daughter's soccer jerseys into a quilt. Another created a family recipe book of favorite holiday recipes, complete with fun quotes from relatives. One mom detailed their family heritage through several generations. Another collected all her daughter's Christmas ornaments given to her since birth and gave them to her for her first adult Christmas in her own home. Creating a life story in photos or videos is one more way to pass along special memories.

As previously mentioned, I began writing letters in a journal to each of my children at their birth and then added a letter on each birthday. Their grandparents and dad also wrote in the journals. When my children turn twenty-one years of age, they receive this journal. Now that one of their grandparents is deceased, these written words have unusually special meaning. I also collected scraps of fabric from clothing that my mother made for my children, and purchased fabrics representative of their favorite hobbies (e.g., dance, baseball, etc.). During each birthday month, I made a quilt square with symbolic fabrics for that year. Sometimes I added pieces of their favorite team jerseys. I have been assembling the squares into quilts, presenting them to each child when they turn twenty-one.

Some resourceful parents plan to publish their rite of passage gifts. Chuck Aquisto celebrated the birth of his first child with writing to more than 1,200 famous, successful people, asking them to share their best advice about life with his son. He wrote one letter a day and then began receiving the responses. Contributors include George Bush, Colin Powell, Bill Cosby, Walter Cronkite, Yogi Berra, and a host of others. He is combining the letters into a book and hopes to use the proceeds to benefit charities.

Kate Marshall created a journal in which family members shared their advice and favorite life tips. This book was given to her daughter on her high school graduation day. A fill-in version will soon be published by Broadway Books, entitled *Words to Live By: A Journal of Life Lessons for Someone You Love.*

Honoring your child's rite of passage into adulthood with an emotional hope chest can be one of life's ultimate celebrations.

Remembering is a variety of imagining and imagining is really a kind of creative remembering.

Stephen Koch

Questions for Reflection

How can you retain a spiritual focus and emphasis on literacy during traditional holiday celebrations?

How can you avoid the pressures of consumerism and commercialism?

Brainstorm about unique rite-of-passage gifts for your children.

Generosity is the soul of writing. You write to give something. To yourself. To your reader. To God. You give thanks for having been given the words. You pray to be given words another day.

Erica Jong

Every word that you write is a blow that smites the devil.

St. Bernard of Clairvaux

You can do anything if you can write. You can defeat any war with imagination.
Ideas are a flowing faucet. You better catch them when they drip.

Janelle Froehlich, ten years old

Chapter 19

In Closing:
The Figurative Hope Chest

People don't commit acts of great evil or great courage out of thin air. Character is developed out of a lifetime of choices.
Ann Coulter

In our culture, hope chests can be literal or figurative. They can be tangible objects or emotional remembrances, passing on to our children what we believe to be important. Our faith is the most powerful hope chest we aim to impart to our children.

With faith at the top of the list, think about what other specific skills you want to pass on to your children to equip them for life. Pursuing this vision requires daily conscious effort.

Our lifetime of choices does affect the future directions of our children. In hindsight, I feel that I was conducting an informal experiment. With our unusual emphasis on family life, I honestly didn't know if our children would become self-consumed isolates or learn to pass our lifestyle on to others. We did try to include friends and relatives in our activities whenever possible.

My three children have enjoyed studying the creative arts. Yet while my older daughter pursued theater and journalism and my son became passionate about music, my younger daughter's similar passions led her down a different path.

From a young age, Natalie was constantly planning parties for her friends. The events became more involved as she became older. Natalie hosted half-birthday parties, valedictorian graduation parties, formal sit-down birthday dinners, mystery dinner theaters, and more events for different friends through the years who she felt needed to be celebrated. She is the child who often added her created holidays to our calendar, including Parent Day and Hippopotamus Day. Natalie kept elaborate planning notebooks for each event, including her own birthday parties.

One Christmas season during her senior year in high school, Natalie and her best friend dressed as elves and delivered ornaments every day for 12 days to 17 friends all around our city, enacting the song, "The Twelve Days of Christmas." Their friend, Hayley, was in the final months of living with cystic fibrosis and would not survive through the year.

On the first day, each friend received a wreath to hang the ornaments on. Natalie and her friend made each ornament to correspond with the verse of the song. Upon delivery, they sang the song up to the verse of the day. On Christmas Day, they sang the entire song as they delivered their final ornament. One day, a friend who lived in an apartment building wasn't home. As Natalie and her friend were about to leave, an elderly woman, who lived across the hall, came out and said, "Don't leave. Everyday I wait by the window for you to come. Will you sing for me?"

On the following St. Patrick's Day, these partners in crime dressed up as leprechauns and sprinkled rainbows of glitter across driveways, leaving pots of golden candy at the end. As a mom, sometimes I would point out that Natalie's time could be much better spent studying for her next exams. Horrified, she would ask, "Is studying more important than making people feel special?" I ate my words as she received an honors scholarship to a fine university. She is pursuing a degree in business.

Children usually will become the embodiment of what is modeled for them. Children who are treated with kindness learn to be kind to others. Children who are spoken to with respect will speak with respect to others. Children who feel loved and treasured learn to treasure others. Children who grow up with celebration will learn to celebrate others in their lives. Children who are raised in richly literate homes will value literacy.

In honor of nurturing your family's writing lifestyle and traditions, a summary of the most important principles found in this book follows.

Twelve Principles for Nurturing the Family Writing Lifestyle

1. *Create a safe environment for writing. Understand what methods block and unblock the writing process.*

2. *Develop a supportive writing group community. Encourage writing buddy relationships.*

3. *Practice immersion in the world of literature.*

4. *Act as a writing mentor and example for your children. Encourage your children to mentor others.*

5. *Offer children choices about what they read and write. Inspire them with high quality models. Explore a variety of genres.*

6. *Encourage children to write throughout each day, keeping journals or life notebooks with them. Offer children opportunities to bring their life experience into their writing.*

7. *Encourage imaginative play and storytelling, while limiting screen time, especially for young children.*

8. *Publish the works of your children so that their writing can be shared with others.*

9. *Help children meet working writers and observe how they approach their craft.*

10. *Integrate other creative arts into the writing process.*

11. *As a family, use writing to problem-solve, process life challenges, and cope with pain. Make writing relevant to daily life.*

12. *Celebrate life through writing. Safeguard relational traditions and spend time communicating as a family.*

Enjoy your family writing adventure!

Section VII

Resources
and Bibliography

Bibliography

Books about writing or writing education (most are cited in this book) are noted with an asterisk.

Adler, Mortimer J. and Charles Van Doren. *How to Read a Book*. New York, NY: Simon & Schuster, 1972.

Angelo, Bonnie. *First Mothers*. New York, NY: William Morrow, 2000.

*Arana, Marie, ed. *The Writing Life: Writers on How They Think and Work*. New York, NY: *The Washington Post*, 2003.

*Atwell, Nancie. *In the Middle: Writing, Reading, and Learning with Adolescents*. Portsmouth, NH: Heinemann, 1987.

Barth, Edna. Series on holiday symbols. New York, NY: Clarion Books.

Baylor, Byrd. *I'm in Charge of Celebrations*. New York, NY: Charles Scribner's Sons, 1986.

Beal, George. *The Independent Book of Anniversaries*. London: Headline, 1992.

*Bender, Sheila. *Keeping a Journal You Love*. Cincinnati, OH: Walking Stick Press, 2001.

Bettelheim, Bruno. *The Uses of Enchantment: The Meaning and Importance of Fairy Tales*. New York, NY: Alfred A. Knopf, 1976.

Birkets, Sven. *The Gutenberg Elegies: The Fate of Reading in an Electronic Age*. New York, NY: Ballantine, 1994.

*Brande, Dorothea. *Becoming a Writer*. Los Angeles, CA: Tarcher, 1981.

*Bumgardner, Joyce. *Helping Students Learn to Write Poetry: An Idea Book for Poets of All Ages*. Boston, MA: Allyn and Bacon, 1997.

Buzan, T. *Use Both Sides of Your Brain*. New York, NY: Dutton, 1974.

*Calkins, Lucy McCormick. *The Art of Teaching Writing*. Portsmouth, NH: Heinemann, 1986.

*———. *Lessons from a Child: On the Teaching and Learning of Writing*. Portsmouth, NH: Heinemann, 1983.

*———. *Living Between the Lines*. Portsmouth, NH: Heinemann, 1991.

*———. *Raising Lifelong Learners: A Parents' Guide*. Reading, MA: Perseus Books, 1997.

*Cameron, Julia. *The Artist's Way: A Spiritual Path to Higher Creativity*. New York, NY: C. P. Putnam, 1992.

*————. *The Right to Write: An Invitation and Initiation into the Writing Life*. New York, NY: Tarcher/Putnam, 1998.

*Canfield, Jack, Mark Victor Hansen and Bud Gardner. *Chicken Soup for the Writer's Soul*. Deerfield Beach, FL: Health Communications, 2000.

Christopher, Doris. *Come to the Table: A Celebration of Family Life*. New York, NY: Warner Books, 1999.

*Clay, Marie. *Writing Begins at Home: Preparing Children for Writing Before They Go to School*. Portsmouth, NH: Heinemann, 1988.

Cleary, Beverly. *A Girl From Yamhill*. New York, NY: Morrow, 1988.

Cox, Meg. *The Heart of a Family: Searching America for New Traditions That Fulfill Us*. New York, NY: Random House, 1998.

Curran, Dolores. *Traits of a Healthy Family*. Minneapolis, MN: Winston Press, 1983.

Dahl, Roald. *Boy: Tales of Childhood*. New York, NY: Penguin Books, 1988.

*Daniel, Lois. *How to Write Your Own Life Story: The Classical Guide for the Nonprofessional Writer*. Chicago, IL: Chicago Review Press, 1991.

*DeSalvo, Louise. *Writing as a Way of Healing: How Telling Our Stories Transforms Our Lives*. San Francisco, CA: Harper, 1999.

*Deutsch, Babette. *Poetry Handbook: A Dictionary of Terms*. New York, NY: Harper Collins, 1974.

*Dillard, Annie. *The Writing Life*. New York, NY: Harper Perennial, 1989.

Doherty, William. *The Intentional Family: How to Build Family Ties in Our Modern World*. Boston, MA: Addison-Wesley Publishers, 1997.

*Elbow, Peter. *Writing with Power: Techniques for Mastering the Writing Process*. New York, NY: Oxford University Press, 1981.

*————. *Writing without Teachers*. New York, NY: Oxford University Press, 1973.

Gardner, Howard. *Art, Mind, and Brain: A Cognitive Approach to Creativity*. New York, NY: Basic Books, 1982.

————. *The Arts and Human Development*. New York, NY: Wiley & Sons, 1973.

————. *Frames of Mind: The Theory of Multiple Intelligence*. New York, NY: Harper Collins, 1989.

*Gardner, John. *The Art of Fiction: Notes on Craft for Young Writers*. New York, NY: Vintage Books, 1983.

*Graham, Paula. *Speaking of Journals: Children's Book Writers Talk About Their Diaries, Notebooks, and Sketchbooks*. Honesdale, PA: Boyds Mills, 1999.

*Grant, Janet. *The Young Person's Guide to Becoming a Writer*. Minneapolis, MN: Free

Spirit, 1995.

*Graves, Donald. *Writing: Teachers and Children at Work*. Portsmouth, NH: Heinemann, 1983.

*Goldberg, Natalie. *Writing Down the Bones: Freeing the Writer Within*. London: Shambhala Press, 1986.

Hart, Leslie. *Human Brain, Human Learning*. New York, NY: Basic Books, 1983.

———. *How the Brain Works: A New Understanding of Human Learning, Emotion, and Thinking*. New York, NY: Basic Books, 1975.

*Harwayne, Shelley. *Writing through Childhood: Rethinking Process and Product*. Portsmouth, NH: Heinemann, 2001.

*Hearn, Virginia. *Just as I Am: Journal-Keeping for Spiritual Growth*. Grand Rapids, MI: Fleming Revell/Baker Books, 1994.

*Heffron, Jack. *The Writer's Idea Book*. Cincinnati, OH: Story Press, 1994.

*Henderson, Kathy. *The Market Guide for Young Writers*. Cincinnati, OH: Writer's Digest Books, 1996.

*Hensley, Dennis. *How to Write What You Love and Make a Living at It*. Colorado Springs, CO: Waterbrook Press, 2000.

Hopkins, Lee Bennett. *Let Them Be Themselves: Language Arts Enrichment for Disadvantaged Children in Elementary Schools*. New York, NY: Harper Collins, 1992.

Hunt, Gladys M. *Honey for a Child's Heart: The Imaginative Use of Books in Family Life*. Grand Rapids, MI: Zondervan, 1978.

Janeczko, Paul. *The Place My Words Are Looking For: What Poets Say About and Through Their Work*. New York, NY: Simon & Schuster, 1990.

Jensen, Eric. *Arts with the Brain in Mind*. Alexandria, VA: Association for Supervision and Curriculum Development, 2001.

*Kaye, Peggy. *Games for Writing: Playful Ways to Help Your Children Learn to Write*. New York, NY: Noonday Press, 1995.

*Kilpatrick, James. *The Writer's Art*. New York, NY: Universal Press, 1984.

*King, Steven. *On Writing: A Memoir of the Craft*. New York, NY: Scribner, 2000.

*Klauser, Henriette Anne. *Put Your Heart on Paper: Staying Connected in a Loose-Ends World*. New York, NY: Bantam Books, 1995.

*———. *Writing on Both Sides of the Brain: Breakthrough Techniques for People Who Write*. New York, NY: Harper Collins, 1987.

*———. *Write It Down, Make It Happen: Knowing What You Want and Getting It*. New York, NY: Simon & Schuster, 2000.

*Koch, Stephen. *The Modern Library Writer's Workshop: A Guide to the Craft of Writing Fiction*. New York, NY: Modern Library/Random House, 2003.

*Korty, Carol. *Writing Your Own Plays: Creating, Adapting, Improvising*. New York, NY: Scribner, 1986.

Krane, Gary. *Simple Fun for Busy People: 333 Ways to Enjoy Your Loved Ones More in the Time You Have*. New York, NY: Fine Communications, 1998.

*Lamott, Anne. *Bird by Bird: Some Instructions on Writing and Life*. New York, NY: Anchor Books, 1995.

Levine, Mel. *A Mind at a Time*. New York, NY: Simon & Schuster, 2002.

Lewis, C. S. *Letters To An American Lady*. Grand Rapids, MI: Eerdmans Publishers, 1967.

Lieberman, Susan. *New Traditions: Redefining Celebrations for Today's Family*. New York, NY: Noonday Press, 1991.

*Livingston, Myra Cohn. *Poem-making: Ways to Begin Writing Poetry*. New York, NY: Harper Collins, 1991

*Lloyd, Pamela. *How Writers Write*. Melbourne, Victoria: Thomas Nelson, 1987.

Margulies, N. *Mapping Inner Space: Learning and Teaching Mindmapping*. Chicago, IL: Zephyr Press, 1991.

Maugham, W. Somerset. *A Writer's Notebook*. New York, NY: Arno Press, 1977.

*Miller, Patti. Writing Your Life: A Journey of Discovery Workshops & Anthology. Allen & Unwin Pty Limited. Crows Nest, N.S.W. Australia. 2001.

*Murray, Donald. *Write to Learn*. New York, NY: Harcourt Brace College Publishers, 1984.

*———. *Read to Write: A Writing Process Reader*. New York, NY: Harcourt Brace College Publishers, 1993.

*———. *Shoptalk: Learning to Write with Writers*. Portsmouth, NH: Heinemann, 1990.

*O'Conner, Patricia T. *Woe is I*. New York, NY: Putnam, 1996.

O'Connor, Flannery. Sally Fitzgerald, ed. *The Habit of Being: Letters of Flannery O'Connor*. New York, NY: Vintage Books, 1980.

*———. *Words Fail Me: What Everyone Who Writes Should Know About Writing*. New York, NY: Harcourt Brace, 1999.

Paterson, Katherine. *A Sense of Wonder*. New York, NY: Penguin Books, 1995.

*———. *Gates of Excellence: On Reading and Writing Books for Children*. New York, NY: Elsevier Books, 1977.

Pipher, Mary, Ph.D. *The Shelter of Each Other*. New York, NY: Grosset/Putnam, 1996.

*Progoff, Ira. *At a Journal Workshop: The Basic Text and Guide for Using the Intensive Journal Process*. Los Angeles, CA: Jeremy Tarcher, 1992.

*Reeves, Judy. *A Writer's Book of Days: A Spirited Companion and Lively Muse for the Writing Life*. Novato, CA: New World Library, 1999.

*————. *Writing Alone, Writing Together: A Guide for Writers and Writing Groups*. Novato, CA: New World Library, 2002.

*Rico, Gabriele Lusser, Ph.D. *Writing the Natural Way: Using Right-Brain Techniques to Release Your Expressive Powers*. New York, NY: G.P. Putnam, 1983.

*————. *Pain and Possibility: Writing Your Way Through Personal Crisis*. Los Angeles, CA: Jeremy Tarcher, 1991.

*Rhodes, Richard. *How to Write: Advice and Reflections*. New York, NY: William Morrow, 1995.

*Rosenthal, Lisa, ed. *The Writing Group Book: Creating and Sustaining a Successful Writing Group*. Chicago, IL: Chicago Review Press, 2003.

*Safire, William and Safir, Leonard. *Good Advice on Writing*. New York, NY: Simon and Schuster, 1992.

* Schneider, Pat. *Writing Alone and with Others*. Oxford University Press. New York, NY 2003.

Smith, Frank. *Insult to Intelligence: The Bureaucratic Invasion of Our Classrooms*. Portsmouth, NH: Heinemann, 1986.

————. *Reading Without Nonsense*. New York, NY: Teachers College Press, 1984.

————. *to think*. New York, NY: Teachers College Press, 1990.

*————. *Writing and the Writer*. Hillsdale, NJ: Lawrence Erlbaum, 1994.

*Stegner, Wallace. *On Teaching and Writing Fiction*. New York, NY: Penguin Books, 2002.

*Stillman, Peter. *Families Writing*. New York, NY: Writer's Digest Books, 1989.

*Strunk, William and White, E.B. *The Elements of Style*. New York, NY. Macmillan, 1979.

Suzuki, Shinichi. *Ability Development from Age Zero*. Athens, OH: Ability Development, 1981.

————. *Nurtured by Love: The Classic Approach to Talent Education*. Smithtown, NY: Exposition, 1973.

————. *Where Love is Deep*. Athens, OH: Ability Development, 1982.

*Thoene, Bodie and Brocke. *Writer to Writer*. Minneapolis, MN: Bethany House, 1990.

*Thomas, Frank. *How to Write the Story of Your Life*. Cincinnati, OH: Writer's Digest

Books, 1984.

Trelease, Jim. *Hey! Listen to This, Stories to Read Aloud.* New York, NY: Penguin Books, 1992.

*Truss, Lynne. *Eats, Shoots & Leaves.* New York, NY: Gotham Books, 2003.

*Ueland, Brenda. *If You Want to Write: A Book About Art, Independence, and Spirit.* St. Paul, MN: Graywolf Press, 1987.

*Vogler, Christopher. *The Writer's Journey.* Studio City, CA: Michael Wiese, 1992.

*Welty, Eudora. *One Writer's Beginnings.* Cambridge, MA: Harvard University Press, 1983.

Wycoff, J. *Mindmapping: Your Personal Guide to Exploring Creativity and Problem-Solving.* New York, NY: Berkeley Books, 1991.

*Zinsser, William. *Inventing the Truth: The Art and Craft of Memoir.* New York, NY: Houghton Mifflin, 1998.

*———. *On Writing Well: The Classic Guide to Writing Nonfiction.* New York, NY: Harper & Row, 1976.

*———. *Writing to Learn.* New York, NY: Harper & Row, 1988.

Recommended Books and Magazines About Writing

Books About Writing:

Each book listed in the bibliography is unique, valuable, and helpful. Because the bibliography is lengthy, the following lists are intended to help you begin reading about the writing process. Authors are listed in alphabetical order. Publishing information can be found in the bibliography.

Books about Writing Education

Atwell, Nancie. *In the Middle—Writing, Reading, and Learning with Adolescents*

Calkins, Lucy McCormick. *The Art of Teaching Writing*

———. *Living Between the Lines*

Elbow, Peter. *Writing with Power*

———. *Writing without Teachers*

Graves, Donald. *Writing: Teachers and Children at Work*

Harwayne, Shelley. *Writing Through Childhood*

Murray, Donald. *Write to Learn*

———. *Shoptalk*

Smith, Frank. *Writing and the Writer*

Books About the Writing Process

Cameron, Julia. *The Artist's Way: A Spiritual Path to Higher Creativity*

———. *The Right to Write: An Invitation and Initiation into the Writing Life*

Dillard, Annie. *The Writing Life*

Goldberg, Natalie. *Writing Down the Bones: Freeing the Writer Within*

Kilpatrick, James. *The Writer's Art*

Klauser, Henriette. *Writing on Both Sides of the Brain*

Koch, Stephen. *The Modern Library Writer's Workshop*

Lamott, Anne. *Bird by Bird: Some Instructions on Writing and Life*

Paterson, Katherine. *Gates of Excellence: On Reading and Writing Books for Children*

Reeves, Judy. *Writing Alone, Writing Together*

Rico, Gabriel Lusser. *Writing the Natural Way*

Rhodes, Richard. *How to Write: Advice and Reflections*

Zinsser, William. *On Writing Well*

————. *Writing to Learn*

Some of my other personal favorites on related writing topics are:

Arana, Marie. *The Writing Life: Writers on How They Think and Work*

DeSalvo, Louise. *Writing as a Way of Healing: How Telling Our Stories Transforms Our Lives*

Klauser, Henriette. *Put Your Heart On Paper*

Rico, Gabriele Lusser. *Pain and Possibility: Writing Your Way Through Personal Crisis*

Rosenthal, Lisa. *The Writing Group Book*

Zinsser, William. *Inventing the Truth: The Art and Craft of Memoir*

Magazines for Writers:

The Writer
Kalmbach Publishing Company
21027 Crossroads Cir.
P. O. Box 1612
Waukesha, WI 53187-1612
customerservice@kalmbach.com

Writer's Digest
4700 E. Galbraith Road
Cincinnati, OH 45236
P. O. Box 420235
Palm Coast, FL 32142
www.writersdigest.com

In addition to their excellent magazines, these publishers offer multiple resources for writers.

Publishers for Young People

Magazines that publish young writers:

Insight Magazine
for teen writers
www.insightmagazine.org

Boodle: By Kids, For Kids
P. O. Box 1049
Portland, IN 47371

Creative Kids
Prufrock Press
P. O. Box 8813
Waco, TX 76714-8813

Kids' World
1300 Kicker Rd.
Tuscaloosa, AL 35404

Merlyn's Pen
For middle school writers
P. O. Box 1058
East Greenwich, RI 02818

Stone Soup
P. O. Box 83
Santa Cruz, CA 95063
www.stonesoup.com

Word Dance Magazine
www.worddance.com

Book publisher for young writers:

Dawn of Day www.dawnofday.com

Best resource for young writers seeking publication:

Locate the latest edition of *The Market Guide for Young Writers* by Kathy Henderson.

A Month of Quotes

Be inspired by these wonderful quotes by famous writers. Use them as writing prompts (a "One-a-Day" writing vitamin for a month) or display them in your office to encourage yourself.

When you write from the heart, you not only light the dark path of your readers, you light your own way as well.

Marjorie Holmes

You must write for children in the same way you do for adults, only better.

Maxim Gorky

A famous poet is a discoverer, rather than an inventor.

Jorge Luis Borges

Don't get it right, get it written.

James Thurber

Writing is the act of burning through the fog in your mind.

Natalie Goldberg

All writers are readers first.

Patricia O'Conner

Creativity does not just shape a product, it shapes a producer.

Frank Smith

Writing is simply the writer and the reader on opposite ends of a pencil; they should be as close together as that.

Jay R. Gould

Writing a book is like rearing children—willpower has very little to do with it. If you have a little baby crying in the middle of the night, and if you depend only on willpower to get you out of bed to feed the baby, that baby will starve. You do it out of love.

Annie Dillard

You don't choose a story, it chooses you. You get together with that story some-how...you're stuck with it.

Robert Penn Warren

Technique alone is never enough. You have to have passion.

Raymond Chandler

Talent is long patience.

Gustave Flaubert

Many writers do little else but sit in small rooms recalling the real world.

Annie Dillard

Writing is my shelter. I don't hide behind the words; I use them to dig inside my heart to find the truth.

Terry McMillan

I believe that what an artist needs most, more than inspiration or financial consolation or encouragement or talent or love or luck, is endurance.

Susan Minot

The pen is the tool of the intuitive. It won't take you further or deeper than you want to go, but it might take you to uncharted places you never thought about consciously.

Judy Reeves

Writing is about getting something down, not about thinking something up.

Julia Cameron

You can learn a great deal about the mechanism of writing in school, but the real picture lies in your understanding of the human heart. No school can teach you that. Only your own ears and eyes.

Howard Fast

No tears in the writer, no tears in the reader. No surprise for the writer, no surprise for the reader. For me the initial delight is in the surprise of remembering something I didn't know I knew.

Robert Frost

The difference between the right word and the almost right word is the difference between lightning and the lightning bug.

Mark Twain

At first people refuse to believe that a strange new thing can be done, then they begin to hope it can be done, then they see it can be done—then it is done and all

the world wonders why it was not done centuries ago.
Frances Hodgson Burnett

Only after the writer lets literature shape her can she perhaps shape literature.
Annie Dillard

My writing is a way to harness my creative energy, while mentally flossing my brain.
Mary Kenyon

Writing is like anything else. You fall, you pick yourself up, and you try again. When you're discouraged, you eat ice cream.
Anna Quindlen

It is the act of writing that calls ideas forward, not ideas that call forward writing.
Julia Cameron

"First do no harm", says the Hippocratic Oath for physicians. If writers of children's books had to take an oath it might begin, "First tell the truth." Children are tougher than adults think they are, and considerably wiser.
William Zinsser

Whoever is devoted to an art must be content to deliver himself wholly up to it and to find his recompense in it.
Charles Dickens

A well-written life is almost as rare as a well-spent one.
Thomas Carlyle

The poet's voice need not merely be the record of man, it can be one of the props, the pillars to help him endure and prevail.
William Faulkner

What a splendid term: fountain pen, the source from which prose flows, except in a dry season.
Edmund Morris

As with many people, Charles, who could not talk, wrote with fullness. He set down his loneliness and his perplexities, and he put on paper many things he did not know about himself.
John Steinbeck,
East of Eden

About the Author:

Author Mary Ann Froehlich, DMA, CCLS, MT-BC, has such an impressive background, that the writing of this book seems natural. After writing nine other books, including *Music Education in the Christian Home* and *What's a Smart Woman Like You Doing in a Place Like This?* and contributing to a variety of professional publications, Mary Ann's literary skills seem to match her musical talents, although she never intended to become a professional writer. With graduate degrees in piano and harp performance and music education/ music therapy, along with a doctorate from the University of Southern California, she is a board certified music therapist and Suzuki music teacher who has specialized in teaching children with special needs. In addition, she has worked with hospitalized and terminally ill children as a certified child life specialist. Mary Ann also has a Master of Arts degree from Fuller Theological Seminary in theology/pastoral care. The mother of three children, Mary Ann resides in California with her husband John.

Printed in the USA
CPSIA information can be obtained
at www.ICGtesting.com
LVHW011258181223
766772LV00010B/393